1998

ANALYSIS FOR MARKETING PLANNING

Third Edition

Donald R. Lehmann
Graduate School of Business
Columbia University

Russell S. Winer
Walter A. Haas School of Business
University of California, Berkeley

IRWIN

Burr Ridge, Illinois
Boston, Massachusetts
Sydney, Australia

TO KRIS, BART, AND KELLY
AND
TO TOBY, JESSICA, AND
ANDREW

 This symbol indicates that the paper in this book is made of
recycled paper. Its fiber content exceeds the recommended
minimum of 50% waste paper fibers as specified by the EPA.

Senior sponsoring editor: Stephen M. Patterson
Editorial coordinator: Lynn Nordbrock
Marketing manager: James Lewis
Project editor: Ethel Shiell
Designer: Larry Cope
Cover designer: Trish Lawrence, Montgomery Media Inc.
Production manager: Bob Lange
Art coordinator: Heather Burbridge
Compositor: Weimer Graphics, Inc.
Typeface: 10/12 Century Schoolbook
Printer: R. R. Donnelley & Sons Company

Library of Congress Cataloging-in-Publication Data

Lehmann, Donald R.
    Analysis for marketing planning / Donald R. Lehmann, Russell S.
Winer.—3rd ed.
        p.   cm.
    Includes index.
    ISBN 0-256-12276-8
    1. Marketing—United States—Management.   I. Winer, Russell S.
II. Title.
HF5415.13.L395   1994
658.8′02—dc20   93–12894

Printed in the United States of America

1 2 3 4 5 6 7 8 9 0   DOC   0 9 8 7 6 5 4 3

THE IRWIN SERIES IN MARKETING

Gilbert A. Churchill, Jr., Consulting Editor
University of Wisconsin, Madison

Alreck & Settle
The Survey Research Handbook
First Edition

Arens & Bovee
Contemporary Advertising
Fifth Edition

Belch & Belch
Introduction to Advertising and Promotion: An Integrated Marketing Communications Approach
Second Edition

Bernhardt & Kinnear
Cases in Marketing Management
Sixth Edition

Bonoma & Kosnik
Marketing Management: Text & Cases
First Edition

Boyd & Walker
Marketing Management: A Strategic Approach
First Edition

Boyd, Westfall, & Stasch
Marketing Research: Text and Cases
Seventh Edition

Burstiner
Basic Retailing
Second Edition

Cadotte
The Market Place: A Strategic Marketing Simulation
First Edition

Cateora
International Marketing
Eighth Edition

Churchill, Ford, & Walker
Sales Force Management
Fourth Edition

Cole
Consumer and Commercial Credit Management
Ninth Edition

Cravens
Strategic Marketing
Fourth Edition

Cravens & Lamb
Strategic Marketing Management Cases
Fourth Edition

Crawford
New Products Management
Fourth Edition

Dillon, Madden, & Firtle
Essentials of Marketing Research
First Edition

Dillon, Madden, & Firtle
Marketing Research in a Marketing Environment
Third Edition

Engel, Warshaw, & Kinnear
Promotional Strategy
Eighth Edition

Faria, Nulsen, & Roussos
Compete
Fourth Edition

Futrell
ABC's of Selling
Fourth Edition

Futrell
Fundamentals of Selling
Fourth Edition

Hawkins, Best, & Coney
Consumer Behavior
Fifth Edition

Berkowitz, Kerin, Hartley, & Rudelius
Marketing
Fourth Edition

Lambert & Stock
Strategic Logistics Management
Third Edition

Lehmann
Market Research and Analysis
Fourth Edition

Lehmann & Winer
Analysis for Marketing Planning
Third Edition

Lehmann & Winer
Product Management
First Edition

Levy & Weitz
Retailing Management
First Edition

Mason, Mayer, & Wilkinson
Modern Retailing
Sixth Edition

Mason, Mayer, & Ezell
Retailing
Fifth Edition

Mason & Perreault
The Marketing Game!
Second Edition

McCarthy & Perreault
**Basic Marketing: A
Global-Managerial
Approach**
Eleventh Edition

McCarthy & Perreault
**Essentials of
Marketing**
Sixth Edition

Patton
Sales Sim
First Edition

Peter & Donnelly
**A Preface to
Marketing
Management**
Sixth Edition

Peter & Donnelly
**Marketing
Management:
Knowledge and Skills**
Third Edition

Peter & Olson
**Consumer Behavior
and Marketing
Strategy**
Third Edition

Peter & Olson
**Understanding
Consumer Behavior**
First Edition

Quelch & Farris
**Cases in Advertising
and Promotion
Management**
Fourth Edition

Quelch, Dolan, & Kosnik
**Marketing
Management:
Text & Cases**
First Edition

Smith & Quelch
Ethics in Marketing
First Edition

Stanton, Buskirk,
& Spiro
**Management of
a Sales Force**
Eighth Edition

Thompson &
Stappenbeck
**The Marketing
Strategy Game**
First Edition

Walker, Boyd,
& Larréché
**Marketing Strategy:
Planning and
Implementation**
First Edition

Weitz, Castleberry,
& Tanner
**Selling: Building
Partnerships**
First Edition

PREFACE

RATIONALE

This book evolved from a course given at the Columbia Business School called Marketing Planning and Strategy. In the mid-1970s, the marketing faculty at Columbia realized that traditional marketing management courses in business school curricula were fine for preparing MBA students for senior-level marketing positions, but did not equip them with the tools necessary for first jobs with such titles as "assistant brand manager" or "assistant account executive." This is because the basic content of marketing management courses is oriented toward the development of marketing strategy that is often the responsibility of the bosses of the newly minted MBAs. It was felt that students needed a more "hands-on" course that would prepare them for the data collection and analysis tasks that often fall to junior-level managers.

The hands-on, practical course that is now required for marketing majors at Columbia and that is being increasingly offered as an elective at other leading business schools is based on the operating, usually annual, marketing plan. The exercise of actually developing a marketing plan is highly integrative as it brings together concepts learned from marketing research, marketing strategy, finance, operations, and policy courses.

This book does not attempt to cover all aspects of the marketing plan. However, we focus on what we feel are the activities most relevant to junior-level managers, that is, the analysis of information pertaining to a product's environment, customers, and competitors. In addition, Chapter 1 contains a complete overview of an operating marketing plan. As such, the book can be used as a companion text to books on strategic marketing management, which tend to focus more on what to do after the type of analysis treated in this book has been completed.

OUTLINE OF THE BOOK

The book has seven major chapters:

1. Overview of Marketing Planning.   In this chapter, we present the rationale for planning, pitfalls that should be avoided, and an outline of a complete marketing plan.
2. Defining Competition.   One of the most challenging decisions faced by marketing managers is that of defining the competition since the set of competitors can usually be constructed as narrowly or as broadly as desired. This chapter discusses methods for defining competiton on different levels of generality.
3. Analyzing Industry Attractiveness.   Fundamental criteria for evaluating a product's position in the market are aggregate factors such as market growth rate, industry factors such as barriers to entry, and environmental factors such as regulation.
4. Competitor Analysis.   Monitoring competitors' strategies and anticipating their future moves is a key to the development of successful marketing strategy. This chapter covers how to analyze competition in terms of competitors' objectives, strategies, and capabilities, and predicting future actions.
5. Customer Analysis.   At the core of modern thinking about marketing is a customer orientation. In this chapter, we discuss the key information required to monitor customer behavior.
6. Market Potential and Forecasting.   In this chapter, we describe methods for estimating the potential size of a market and predicting future levels of sales and/or market share.

These chapters provide discussion of specific analytical methods and data sources that can be useful for each of the analyses discussed in the chapters as well as some useful formats for summarizing the information.

This edition contains a seventh chapter:

7. Integrating Analysis and Strategy.   Rather than leaving the reader "hanging" after the discussion of the situation analysis, we have added a chapter outlining how the concepts developed earlier in the book can be used to develop a marketing strategy.

In preparing this revision, we made a number of changes. These include an updated plan outline (Chapter 1), more discussion on brand switching (Chapter 2), reorganized and expanded industry analysis (Chapter 3), more on product/service comparisons (Chapter 4), a major reworking of Chapter 5 to include brand equity, quality and satisfaction, intentions, and latent class methods, and an extended classification of objectives (Chapter 7).

ACKNOWLEDGMENTS

We would like to acknowledge our former students at Columbia, Vanderbilt, and Berkeley who have stimulated our thoughts and given us incentive to improve our understanding of marketing planning. We have received valuable comments from the reviewers and colleagues at our current schools and other universities. This latter group includes particularly: Mac Hulbert at Columbia; Allan Shocker, University of Minnesota; Kim Corfman and Joel Steckel, New York University; Sharon E. Beatty, University of Alabama; Richard Kolbe, Washington State University; and Ronald Lonsdale, Loyola University of Chicago. Reviewers for the most recent revision were John Van Kirk, Xavier University; John Friar, Northeastern; Michael Morris, University of Central Florida; and Kent Nakamoto, University of Colorado.

We also want to thank Steve Patterson (our "wonderful sponsoring editor" in his own words) of Irwin for his encouragement and good-natured prodding and Lynn Nordbrock for her editorial efforts. As always, we thank our families for their patience. A special thanks goes to Kris Lehmann for her editorial and word processing assistance.

We hope you find the book useful.

Donald R. Lehmann
Russell S. Winer

CONTENTS

CHAPTER 1

OVERVIEW

OVERVIEW

Mention the term *marketing* and many people immediately think of catchy advertising slogans, price promotions, or the dreaded phone solicitation during dinner. While both important and salient, however, these and other tactics are simply manifestations of strategies which in turn are, or at least should be, developed consistent with an analysis of the world outside the firm: industry trends, and competitor and customer behavior. This book focuses on the analyses that guide strategy selection and indirectly the tactics of advertising, pricing, distribution, and so on.

This book is organized around the development of a marketing plan with particular emphasis on annual marketing plans. This provides a format which is useful for organizing discussion and is directly applicable for aiding the systematic development of marketing strategy. This chapter provides a brief overview of marketing planning and a general format for constructing a plan. Recognize, however, that planning is not an end in itself, but rather a means for improving the chances of selecting a sound and profitable strategy.

DEFINITION AND OBJECTIVES OF PLANS

Marketing planning is a major activity in most large firms. One survey (Hulbert, Lehmann, and Hoenig, 1987) found over 90 percent of marketing executives engaged in formal planning. The executives spent an average of 45 days a year in planning, and they relied most heavily on information from the sales force, management information systems, and internal marketing research. The development of plans, which are generally annual in nature and focus on product/product line or market, are thus an important function for marketers, one that is seen as beneficial for improving both coordination and performance.

1

The marketing plan can be divided into two general parts: the situation analysis, and the objectives, strategy, and programs that direct the firm's actions. While most books and the popular press concentrate on the latter, incorrect or inadequate analysis often leads to poor decisions regarding actions. Therefore, this book is devoted to the mundane but critical and surprisingly interesting task of providing the analysis on which to base an action plan—in short, the marketing homework.

Since our objective is to produce a short book, we consciously leave out some important topics. We do not cover detailed financial analysis (e.g., of profitability by product, channel, etc.) because it requires very specific (and often faulty) internal data and promotes to some extent an inward rather than outward orientation. Also, we consider the firm's strengths and weaknesses as part of competitor analysis rather than on their own. We also chose not to focus on program implementation and control procedures because these vary substantially depending on objectives and data availability and because they are applied after a plan and strategy are selected.

This book provides guidelines for preparing the central parts of the background analysis necessary to develop a marketing plan: customer, competitor, and industry analysis, plus planning assumptions and forecasting. Thus, this book takes a niche strategy rather than trying to be all things to all people.

What is a formal **marketing plan?** A working definition is:

> A marketing plan is a *written* document containing the guidelines for the *business unit's* marketing programs and allocations over the *planning period.*

Several parts of the above definition have been emphasized and merit further explanation.

First, note that a formal plan is a *written document,* not something stored in a manager's head. This characteristic of marketing plans produces multiple benefits. It encourages and requires disciplined thinking. It ensures that prior experiences in terms of strategies that succeeded or failed are not lost. It provides a vehicle for communication between functional areas of the firm, such as manufacturing, finance, and sales, which is vital to the successful implementation of a plan. The marketing plan also helps pinpoint responsibility for achieving results by a specified date. Finally, a written plan provides for continuity when there is management turnover and for quickly indoctrinating new employees to the situation facing the business.

A second aspect of the marketing plan definition to note is that it is usually written at the *business unit level.* This is purposely vague because the precise level at which plans are written varies from organization to organization. For example, in a typical brand management-organized company, a marketing plan is written for each brand since it is a profit center.

Alternatively, some companies write plans for groups of brands or services, particularly when direct fixed costs are difficult to allocate by individual product. Thus, it is difficult to provide a general statement of the organizational level at which marketing planning activities operate.

For example, General Foods developed a separate marketing plan for each brand of cereal marketed by the Post division, such as Raisin Bran and Grape Nuts. Alternatively, McDonald's has one overall marketing plan for its fast-food operations, with perhaps some regional differences, since separate menu items such as Chicken McNuggets and the McLean sandwich are integrated into the menu and would not be viewed as distinct brands. In this case, the menu almost acts as the "product" and menu items as product features.

A final item to note from the definition of a marketing plan is that the planning period varies from product to product. Retailing traditionally has short planning cycles to match the seasonality and vagaries of fashion trends. Automobiles, however, have longer planning cycles since lead times for product development and/or modifications are longer. Other factors contributing to variation in the length of planning horizons are rates of technological change, intensity of competition, and frequency of shifts in the tastes of relevant groups of customers. The typical horizon, however, is annual, as supported by data reported in Figure 1–1.

Often, there is confusion between what is termed *strategic* planning and *marketing* planning. We distinguish between them in the following ways. First, strategic planning is usually performed at a higher level in the organization than is marketing planning. Using Figure 1–2 as a guide, strategic planning occurs at the corporate, group, or strategic business unit levels. At these levels, objectives are broad (e.g., return on investment or

FIGURE 1–1

Time Horizons for Marketing Plans

Time Period	Industrial Products	Consumer Products	Service Firms
Less than one year	1%	6%	—%
One year	18	23	14
One year, plus brief reference to later years	44	40	58
One year, plus a separate longer-range plan	18	16	—
More than one year	19	15	28
	100%	100%	100%

Source: David S. Hopkins, *The Marketing Plan* (New York: The Conference Board, 1981), p. 10. © 1981 The Conference Board.

FIGURE 1–2
Hierarchy of Planning

assets) and strategies are general (e.g., divesting manufacturing cans and investing in financial services). At the business center level, marketing plans have specific objectives (market share) and strategies (pursuing the small business segment). A second difference is that strategic plans usually have a longer time horizon than marketing plans; three to five years or more with annual updates is not uncommon.

In summary, the marketing plan is an operational document. While it contains strategies for the business center, it is more short-term oriented than what might be called a strategic plan. Marketing plans are specific statements of how to achieve short-term results.

The objectives of a marketing plan can be stated concisely as:

1. Define the current business situation (and how we got there).
2. Define problems and opportunities facing the business.
3. Establish objectives.
4. Define the strategies and programs necessary to achieve the objectives.
5. Pinpoint responsibility for business center objectives.
6. Establish timetables for achieving objectives.
7. Encourage careful and disciplined thinking.
8. Establish an outward (customer/competitor) orientation.

This last marketing plan objective is particularly relevant for this book. Most managers are aware of the **marketing concept** popularized in the 1960s; this dictates that marketers must maintain a customer orientation in all their strategies. This customer orientation was reinforced during the early 1980s by Peters and Waterman's book *In Search of Excellence* and Tom Peters' numerous television appearances that exhorted managers to keep close to customers. Less commonly acknowledged is that a competitor orientation, especially in today's business environment, is as important. However, a few recent books with titles incorporating the word *warfare* have focused on the competitive nature of marketing. The vast majority of products and services are not monopolies; competitors often determine a brand's profits as much as any action taken by the marketing manager. By emphasizing the importance of having both a customer and competitor orientation, we believe this book focuses on the two most important components of the strategy development process.

Issues in the Planning Process

Unfortunately, not all organizations which developed marketing plans have been pleased with the process. The Strategic Planning Institute has identified common mistakes and issues in strategic planning that seem relevant to marketing planning as well.

The Speed of the Process
There is the problem of either being so slow that the process seems to go on continuously or so fast that there is an extreme burst of activity to rush out a plan. In the former case, managers become "burned out" by constantly filling out forms that can distract them from operational tasks. In the latter case, a quickly developed plan can easily lead to critical oversights.

The Amount of Data Collected
Sufficient data are needed to properly estimate customer needs and competitive trends. However, the law of diminishing returns quickly sets in on the data-collection process. A small percentage of all the data available usually produces a large percentage of the insights obtainable. We hope this book will be useful in describing the data considered most essential.

Who Does the Planning?
In the late 1960s, strategic planning models developed by the Boston Consulting Group, McKinsey, General Electric, and others led to the formation of formal strategic planning groups in many major corporations. Essentially, the planning process was delegated to the professional planners, while implementation of the plans was left to the line managers. Naturally, line managers resented this process; they thought the planners had no "feel" for the markets for which they were planning and were managing

totally by the numbers rather than including any market intuition gleaned from experience. As a result, hostility grew between the staff planners and line managers to the point where recommended strategies were either poorly implemented or ignored. Now, because of both poor results from staff-directed planning efforts and the recent recessions, which led to large cuts in corporate staffs, line managers are much more involved with planning, both strategic and marketing (*Business Week,* 1984). The conclusion seems to be that line managers should develop marketing plans but with staff assistance.

The Structure

Clearly, any formal planning effort involves some structure. Structure forces discipline on the planners; that is, certain data must be collected. Many executives believe the most important result of planning is not the plan itself but the structuring of thought about the strategic issues facing the business. However, the structure should not take precedence over the content so planning becomes mere form filling or number crunching. Still, while the process should not be too bureaucratic, there must be enough structure to force completion. A good solution to the dilemma is to consider the plan format as a guide but with a rigid timetable. Flexibility in format helps to prevent the plan from being mindless paper shuffling.

Length of Plan

The length of a marketing plan must be balanced between being so long it is ignored by both line and senior managers and so brief that it ignores key details. Many organizations have formal guidelines for the optimal lengths of documents (e.g., Procter & Gamble's one-page limit on memos); what is long for one firm may be optimal for another. A modal length, however, is about 20 to 50 pages.

Frequency of Planning

A common mistake is to plan either more frequently or less frequently than necessary. Too frequent reevaluation of strategies can lead to erratic firm behavior. Also, the planning process becomes more burdensome than necessary. However, when plans are not revised frequently enough, the business may not adapt quickly enough to environmental changes and thus suffer a deterioration in its competitive position. Environmental conditions such as tax returns and reporting requirements tend to favor an annual plan.

Number of Alternative Strategies Considered

Discussing too few alternatives raises the likelihood of failure, while discussing too many increases the time and cost of the planning effort. Multiple alternatives should be considered, but this does not mean all marketing personnel need to be heard. It is important to have diversity in the strategic options (e.g., both growth and hold strategies) since discarded strategies often prove useful as contingency plans.

Cross-Functional Acceptance

Successful implementation of a marketing plan requires a broad consensus including other functional areas. For example, a high-quality strategy is difficult to implement if manufacturing does not simultaneously exert high-quality control. Growth objectives may be achievable only through the relaxation of credit policies. A common mistake is to view the plan as a proprietary possession of marketing management.

Using the Plan as a Sales Document

A major but often overlooked purpose of a plan and its presentation is to generate funds from either internal sources (i.e., to gain budget approval) or external sources (i.e., to gain a partner for a joint venture). To state it differently, the plan and its proponents compete with other plans and their proponents for scarce resources. Therefore, the more appealing the plan and the better the track record of its proponents, the better the chance of budget approval.

THE PLANNING PROCESS

Approaches to Planning

Two general approaches to planning have developed. In "top-down" planning, the marketing plans are formulated either by senior or middle management with the aid of staff and implemented by lower-echelon personnel such as sales representatives. An alternative to such top-down approaches are "bottom-up" planning methods in which the lower ranks are actively involved in providing forecasts and collecting competitor and customer information. The information is subject to higher-level review, but in such a planning system, the lower management personnel play a key role in the process.

Both systems have some commendable characteristics. The rationale often used for top-down planning is that people higher up in the organization have a better perspective of the context of problems facing the business. Field salespeople, for example, tend to consider the competitive battleground as their sales territory and not necessarily the national or international market. Bottom-up planning systems are often characterized by better implementation than top-down approaches because the people primarily charged with executing the plan are involved in its development; this is consistent with the current trend toward employee empowerment.

Steps in the Planning Process

In most organizations, the planning process involves a programmed sequence of events. These events generally follow the seven steps listed below and shown in Figure 1–3.

FIGURE 1–3
Marketing Planning Sequence

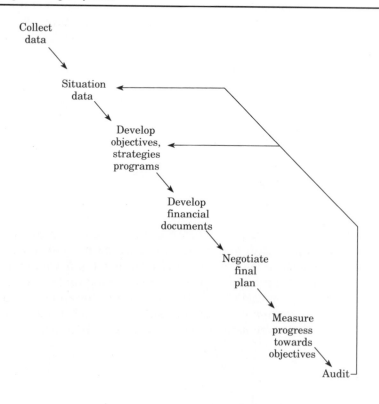

Step 1. Collecting Background Data. The data-collection effort focuses on information available on the past and current situations. Data collected for marketing planning are often either provisional or estimated. For example, in planning for 1991, actual market size data for 1990 may not be available, but forecasts for 1990 developed in 1989 are often available. Also, preliminary estimates of the gross national product (GNP) for 1990 may exist but not the final figures.

Step 2. Analyzing Historical and Background Data. Existing data are analyzed to forecast competitors' actions, customers' behavior, economic conditions, and so forth. Such an analysis (termed the *situation analysis*) need not be quantitative; in fact, much of the analysis, as will be seen in later chapters, is qualitative with emphasis on drawing implications from nonnumerical data. This analysis leads to the delineation of key opportunities and threats to the business.

Step 3. Developing Objectives, Strategies, and Action Programs. The implications drawn from the background data (see Step 2) are used to formulate product objectives, strategies, and marketing mix decisions. This is the critical activity of the planning process because it outlines in detail what will be done with the product during the year (or appropriate planning period). However, the order of the steps indicates that logical strategic thinking cannot be done without considering the facts.

The objectives, strategies, and mix decisions are constrained by company mission, objectives and strategy, company policy and resources, and legal considerations, among other factors. Thus, this part of the process generally involves (*a*) setting objectives, (*b*) developing strategies and programs to achieve the objectives, (*c*) comparing the programs in terms of their ability to achieve objectives (e.g., profit) *and* to be acceptable in terms of company policy and legal constraints, and (*d*) selecting a basic objective, strategy, and program combination.

Step 4. Developing Pro Forma Financial Statements. Such statements typically include budgets and profit and loss (income) figures.

Step 5. Negotiating. Rarely, if ever, is the market plan generated from Steps 1 to 4 implemented without several rounds of negotiations with senior management. In a brand management organizational structure, the plans themselves must be marketed as managers vie for corporate resources. In large organizations, this negotiation phase can last as long as all the prior steps.

Step 6. Measuring Progress. In order to make necessary corrections to the plan as the environment changes within the planning period, the progress of the plan toward the stated objectives must be monitored. Thus, marketing research and other information relevant to measuring the quantities stated as objectives (e.g., market share and sales) must be collected on an interim basis.

Step 7. Auditing. After a planning period, it is customary to review results to determine variances of planned versus actual results and sources of the variances. This audit provides important diagnostic information for both current and future planning efforts and thus acts as a source of feedback to the planning effort.

The planning sequence is therefore a logical flow of events leading from data collection and analysis to strategy formulation to auditing the performance of the plan. It implies that sound strategic thinking cannot occur until the planner has sufficiently utilized available information to draw implications about future market conditions.

COMPONENTS OF THE MARKETING PLAN

While nearly every firm has its own format (see Hopkins, 1981, for examples), most marketing plans have a common set of elements. A sample of a complete marketing plan outline is provided as an appendix to this chapter and is summarized in Figure 1–4. This outline describes the major areas of analysis and data collection required for a typical marketing plan. The rationale and a brief description of each major component of the plan are of-

FIGURE 1–4
Marketing Plan Summary

  I. Executive summary
 II. Situation analysis
     A. Industry analysis
     B. Sales analysis
     C. Competitor analysis
     D. Customer analysis
     E. Planning assumptions
     F. Forecasts
III. Marketing objectives
 IV. Marketing strategy
  V. Marketing programs
 VI. Financial documents
VII. Monitors and controls
VIII. Contingency plans

---

fered below to give an overview of the plan and the context in which this book is set.

The Executive Summary

A senior manager often must review many marketing plans. In such situations, a brief summary of the marketing plan focusing on the objectives, strategies, and expected financial performance is mandatory. This summation provides a quick overview of the major elements of the plan and easier comparison between product plans.

Situation Analysis

1. Industry Analysis seeks to identify long-term trends and short-term changes in the market. This section applies to past data; that is, if we are planning for 1991 in 1990, historical data will include 1989 and older information. The major areas of interest include general market data, such as sales and market shares; market activity information, such as advertising and pricing histories; historical cost and profit data; and facts related to changes in technology, regulations, or other general environmental conditions. Since this data becomes voluminous over time, it is often stored in a separate document called a Product Fact Book.

The Product Fact Book is a separate but related part of the overall marketing plan comprising the statistical and permanent record of product and market results, activities, conditions, and characteristics. Its purpose is to:

   a. Provide a ready reference for all necessary information that forms the basis of the marketing plan.
   b. Permit the basic part of the marketing plan to be relatively brief in form and operational in usage.
   c. Provide a fast and easy way for new personnel to become acquainted with the product and market. (This is especially pertinent in view of management policy fostering transfers.)

Primary responsibility for preparation and maintenance of the Product Fact Book is usually assumed by the senior marketing manager for a product/ product line.

The industry analysis also identifies factors that can be used to assess the attractiveness of an industry in which the firm is competing. Since all markets are dynamic in that competitors, customers, technology, and sales growth rates change, the underlying attractiveness of an industry as a target for investment also changes.

2. *Sales Analysis* is an intensive study of a brand's sales records intended to uncover problems hidden by aggregate numbers. For example, an overall sales increase of a line of shoes may be hiding the fact that sales of a particular size or color are dropping or unprofitable.

3. *Competitor Analysis* addresses the question: What are the key competitors in the market likely to do in the future? Since virtually all markets are competitive, it is easy to see why this is a vital section. This includes engineering-based comparison of both competitors' product capabilities and their sales levels. Also relevant is a competitor analysis of the brand for which the plan is being written. In other words, strengths and weaknesses of the brand of interest are determined by comparison to those of the major competitors.

4. *Customer Analysis* attempts to guarantee the customer orientation that is critical to the success of the product. It is vital to understand not only who the customers are but also how and why they behave as they do.

5. *Planning Assumptions* involve a wide variety of quantities. For example, market potential for the product is a key number since it affects expected future category growth, resource allocation, and many other constructs related to decision making. Assumptions are also made about uncontrollable factors, such as raw materials or labor supply.

6. *Forecasts* of both industry and product sales are also relevant for this section.

The situation analysis thus forms the "homework" part of the plan necessary before marketing objectives and strategies can be properly formulated. While it is perhaps more enjoyable to develop concepts of where a business should go during the next planning horizon, up-front data collection and analysis are the most vital part of the plan; time spent drawing implications from the background data often makes the optimal strategies relatively apparent.

The Marketing Strategy Section

It is logical that the situation analysis precede the strategy portion of the plan. This part actually comprises three sections: a statement of marketing objectives ("Where do we want to go?"), the marketing strategy ("Generally, how are we going to get there?"), and the marketing programs consisting of the marketing mix elements ("Exactly what do we do in what order?").

The Rest of the Plan

The final three parts of the marketing plan do not form a cohesive unit but are vital components. The financial documents report the budgets and pro forma profit and loss (income) statements. Senior managers inspect the expected financial outcome with extreme care. In fact, the P&L statements are often the key "sales document" in securing approval for the plan. The monitors and controls section specifies the type of marketing research and other information necessary to measure progress toward achieving the stated objectives. The kind of information usually collected depends on the objectives; for example, if a market share increase is the objective, then such information must be collected in a timely manner to check for possible shortfalls. Finally, contingency plans are helpful, particularly in dynamic markets where either new products or competitors often create the need for strategy changes before the end of the plan's horizon. Often, these contingencies are previously considered strategies, discarded for some reason.

SUMMARY

A marketing plan can thus be seen as a cohesive device intended to act as a guideline for the allocation of resources for a product. While there are many good references for the development of strategy, relatively few sources exist for a description of the background analysis necessary prior to strategy formulation. This book thus emphasizes the homework part of marketing planning activities.

We aim to be as complete as possible with each topic in taking a how-to orientation. We discuss the steps necessary to conduct the analyses, provide illustrations of approaches taken, and describe some sources of information typically used to perform the analyses. In doing so, we often use many examples from consumer packaged goods. This does not indicate that the material applies primarily to consumer goods; it applies as well to industrial goods and services. Our choice of examples is dictated by the desire to be understandable to most readers; hence food or clothing serves our pedagogical purposes better than oil well drilling equipment or financial hedging investments.

Since much of the situation analysis presumes a definition of the industry in which a product is competing, we begin by describing methods for defining the competitive set. Once that has been established, Chapter 3 discusses industry analysis. Chapter 4 describes how competitors can be analyzed with an eye toward predicting their likely future strategies. In Chapter 5, we describe approaches for analyzing customers, including methods for identifying market segments. The role of planning assumptions, market potential, and forecasting are detailed in Chapter 6, while in the concluding chapter, we describe the results of putting together all the data, developing marketing strategies.

APPENDIX: MARKETING PLAN OUTLINE

The following is a possible outline for developing a marketing plan. The upcoming chapters provide more detail on the situation analysis and objectives and strategies sections.

- I. Executive Summary. A one- to three-page synopsis of the plan providing highlights of the current situation, objectives, strategies, principal action programs, and financial expectations.
- II. Situation Analysis.
    - A. Industry analysis.
        1. Market.
            - a. Size, scope, and share of the market sales history of all producers and their market shares.
            - b. Market potential and major trends in supply and demand of this and related products.
        2. Market activity.
            - a. Pricing history through all levels of distribution and reasons for principal fluctuations.
            - b. The distribution channels.
            - c. Selling policies and practices.
            - d. Advertising and promotion.
        3. Sales, costs, and gross profits.
            - a. Sales history by grades, varieties; by sales district; by end use; by industry.
            - b. Cost history.
            - c. Profit history.
            - d. Changes in volume and profit rankings of product lines and items in a product line.
        4. Technology—Product and process improvements.
            - a. Rate (life cycle).
            - b. Lead time required for design and development of a new product.
            - c. Market impact (primary versus selective demand).
            - d. How interrelated are product and process?
        5. Market characteristics: Trends in.
            - a. Industry use patterns.
            - b. End-use patterns.
            - c. Frequency, quantity, and timing of purchase.
            - d. Buying procedures and practices.
            - e. Service.

6. Government and social.
   a. Regulatory climate.
   b. Fiscal and monetary policy.
   c. Consumerism.
   d. Environmental impact.
7. Industry attractiveness analysis.
   a. Market factors:
      (1) Size.
      (2) Growth.
      (3) Cyclicity.
      (4) Seasonality.
   b. Industry factors:
      (1) Capacity.
      (2) New product entry prospects.
      (3) Rivalry.
      (4) Power of suppliers.
      (5) Power of buyers.
      (6) Threat of substitutes.
   c. Environmental factors:
      (1) Social.
      (2) Political.
      (3) Demographic.
      (4) Technological.
      (5) Regulatory.
B. Sales analysis.
   1. Market area performance versus company average.
   2. Trends of sales, costs, and profits by products.
   3. Performance of distributors, end users, key customers.
   4. Past versus current results by area, product, channel, and so on.
C. Competitor analysis.
   1. For each major competitor and your own company, ask:
      a. How does he measure and evaluate his results?
      b. How did he achieve the results and what factors helped or hurt him?
      c. What are his important strengths and liabilities and how are these likely to change?
      d. What is his future strategy likely to be?
   2. Thorough analysis requires:
      a. Exploration of past results.
      b. Reconstruction of past strategy.
      c. Evaluation of resources.
         (1) Ability to conceive and design new products.
         (2) Ability to produce or manufacture.
         (3) Ability to market.
         (4) Ability to finance.
         (5) Ability to manage.
         (6) Will to succeed in this business.
      d. Comparative analysis of existing and anticipated future products.
D. Customer analysis—key questions to better understand your market.
   1. Who:
      a. Who are your customers?

       b. How can they be classified?

       c. Which classification is most important to you and your competitors—today and tomorrow?

    2. Why:

       a. Why do customers buy when, as much as, and the way they do?

       b. How involved and prolonged is the purchase decision?

       c. How many people are involved and at what level?

       d. What are the objectives of each person involved?

       e. Which objectives are most important?

    3. What if . . .

       a. What would cause a change in customers' objectives?

       b. What information will help anticipate these changes?

    4. So what?

       a. What are the implications of changes in customer behavior?

       b. What is the expected impact on you and your competitors?

    5. What then?

       a. How will this customer analysis improve your understanding of the total market, size, mix growth rate, and timing?

  E. Planning assumptions.

    1. Explicit statement of assumptions about the future.

    2. Projections, predictions, and forecasts.

  F. Forecasts.

    1. Industry.

    2. Product.

III. Objectives.

  A. Corporate objectives (if appropriate).

  B. Divisional objectives (if appropriate).

  C. Marketing objectives.

    1. Quantity (sales, share, and so on).

    2. Direction.

    3. Number.

    4. Time frame.

    5. Rationale.

  D. Program objectives.

    1. Pricing.

    2. Advertising/promotion.

    3. Sales/distribution.

    4. Product.

    5. Service.

IV. Marketing Strategy: How the objectives will be achieved.

  A. Strategic alternative(s).

  B. Customer targets.

  C. Competitor targets.

  D. Core strategy.

V. Marketing Programs.

  A. Pricing.

  B. Advertising/promotion.

    1. Copy.

    2. Media.

    3. Trade versus consumer promotion.

  C. Sales/distribution.

    D. Product development.
    E. Service.
    F. Market research.
 VI. Financial Documents.
    A. Budgets.
      1. Advertising/promotion.
      2. Sales.
      3. Research.
      4. Product development.
    B. Pro forma statements.
      1. Costs.
        a. Dollar, unit.
        b. Variable, fixed.
      2. Revenues (forecasted).
      3. Profits.
        a. Dollars, dollars per unit.
        b. ROI.
        c. Versus company average.
 VII. Monitors and Controls: Specific research information to be used.
    A. Secondary data.
      1. Sales reports.
      2. Orders.
      3. Informal sources.
    B. Primary data.
      1. Sales records (Nielsen, IRI).
      2. Specialized consulting firms.
      3. Customer panel.
VIII. Contingency Plans and Other Miscellaneous Documents.
    A. Contingency plans.
    B. Alternative strategies considered.
    C. Miscellaneous.

REFERENCES

Hopkins, David. *The Marketing Plan.* New York: The Conference Board, 1981.

Hulbert, James M.; Donald R. Lehmann; and Scott Hoenig. "Practices and Impacts of Marketing Planning." Working paper, Graduate School of Business, Columbia University, 1987.

"The New Breed of Strategic Planner." *Business Week,* September 17, 1984, pp. 62–66; 68.

Peters, Thomas J., and Robert H. Waterman, Jr. *In Search of Excellence.* New York: Warner Books, 1982.

Sutton, Howard. *The Marketing Plan in the 1990s.* New York: The Conference Board, 1990.

CHAPTER 2

DEFINING THE COMPETITIVE SET

OVERVIEW

Perhaps the most basic component of a marketing orientation is an outward orientation. This orientation principally focuses on customers, competitors, and the general environment for the industry (e.g., growth prospects, suppliers, regulation). These three components are interrelated: who the competitors are helps define the industry and customers, analysis of customers helps define who the competitors are, and industry characteristics suggest likely competitive strategies. Consequently, analyses of the customers, competitors, and industry are interdependent, and which comes first is a bit of a "chicken and egg" issue. Here we somewhat nontraditionally begin with a focus on the industry and competition and then discuss customer analysis. One benefit of this approach is that customers are then necessarily viewed more broadly than as customers of the particular companies' offerings, in essence a minor guarantee against a myopic view of the world.

More specifically, we begin with a discussion of how to define the firm's product/service competitors. We address the "who do we or will we compete with" question to better understand what industry we are in, to select which competitors to analyze (i.e., in terms of financial strength), and to inform our customer analysis. For short-run plans in a mature market, most of the focus is usually on competitors with similar offerings targeted to the same customers (what we later define as product form and product category competitors). This chapter takes a broader, more long-run view to help avoid being caught by a major technological shift (e.g., computers substituting for typewriters) and to encourage a more long-run orientation.

The purpose of this chapter is to help marketing managers determine the identity of the "enemy." A distinct precondition to both analyzing competitors' capabilities and developing competitive strategy is the assessment of the sources of competitive threat.

Consider the following quote from *Advertising Age* attributed to a copywriter at Ted Bates:

A Bates writer can't write until someone points out the enemy. . . . If your share goes up, somebody else's share must go down. I want to know that somebody else. . . . Many categories have stopped growing, so it's more important than ever to know where you're going to get your customers.

In some sense, everything competes with everything else. The key question, therefore, is not whether products or services compete but the extent to which they compete. Defining competition requires a balance between identifying too many competitors (complicating instead of simplifying decision making) and identifying too few (and overlooking one or more key competitors).

Although the competitive arena usually involves the fight for customers, competitors tangle on other bases, too. For example, IBM and Emerson Electric, noncompetitors in terms of customers, compete for electrical engineers from the same labor supply. Kodak and jewelers compete for silver, that is, raw materials. Avon and Tupperware compete for home demonstration sales and salespeople: the same channel of distribution. Similarly, all manufacturers that sell through supermarkets and department stores compete for shelf space. Geographically based competition is important for both local retailers, such as hardware stores, and multinational firms, such as Ericsson (Sweden), NEC (Japan), and Northern Telecom (Canada) in the telecommunications equipment market. In other words, competition exists in many dimensions. Therefore, it is important to consider many types of competition as listed in Figure 2–1.

As this figure suggests, competitors can be defined using several criteria. Competition can exist for customers in terms of their budgets (disposable income: vacations versus financial products), when they use a product (evenings: a basketball game versus a personal improvement

FIGURE 2–1
Bases of Competition

I. Customer-oriented
  Who they are—competition for same budget
  When they use it
  Why they used it—benefits sought
II. Marketing-oriented: advertising and promotion
  Theme/copy strategy
  Media
  Distribution
  Price
III. Resource-oriented
  Raw materials
  Employees
  Financial resources
IV. Geographic

---

seminar), and benefits sought (cancer treatments: bioengineered drugs versus chemotherapy). Competition is also related to marketing activities such as advertising (time on network television programs) and distribution (shelf space). The battle for shelf facings in supermarkets has led to a variety of manufacturer concessions to retailers to obtain desirable shelf positions, and the struggle for shelf space occurs across and within product category boundaries. Companies compete for resources, including both raw materials and personnel. Firms in the same geographic area compete for attention and sales dollars.

Perhaps the most crucial competition occurs *within* a company, when different units in an organization ask for funds. In this competition, the marketing plan acts mainly as a sales document, and its financial projections often become the key to the sale. This competition is often intentional because it pressures product managers to develop sound and ambitious marketing plans.

Misidentification of the competitive set can have a serious impact on the success of a marketing plan, especially in the long run. One problem is that an important competitive threat can be overlooked. For example, the Swiss controlled the market for premium watches and Timex the market for inexpensive watches for many years. When the Japanese firms developed electronic watches in the 1970s, they were not viewed as a threat or serious competition to either business. History, of course, tells a different story; Timex was forced to develop electronic watches, while the Swiss added lines using electronic works.

Similarly, steelmakers only slowly reacted to the intrusion of plastics into the automobile market. Such an acknowledgment years ago would have produced new products with the lighter-weight advantage of plastics and, perhaps, prevented or at least slowed the steel industry's decline.

As a third example, some of the decline in the coffee market has been due to increased competition from other beverages, particularly in the morning segment. Orange juice manufacturers have spent increasing sums on advertising and product development. Even soft drink manufacturers want some of the action; Pepsi developed Pepsi A.M. to compete squarely with coffee.

Moreover, ambiguous definition of the competition creates uncertainty in market definition and, therefore, market-related statistics such as market share. This leaves open the possible manipulation of market boundaries, particularly when compensation or allocation decisions are at stake. For example, assume an objective for Pepsi A.M. is to gain a 10 percent market share. The ability to achieve this objective depends on whether Pepsi A.M. competes in the soft drink market, the cola market, the caffeine beverage market, or the morning beverage market. Thus, deciding in which market you wish to compete is important for both developing and controlling marketing effort.

In this chapter, therefore, we take the view that the definition of the competitive set ultimately affects what strategy is pursued. Not all authors subscribe to this approach. Abell (1980), for example, believes the corporate mission or business definition affects the set of competitors against which a firm fights. Unfortunately, competitors usually do not care how a company defines itself and are free to compete against a firm's brands even if that firm does not define itself in a way that would include a certain set of brands or companies as competitors.

In this chapter, we present several levels of competition that can help conceptualize the competitive set. In addition, we discuss methods that can be employed to determine the competition at the various levels. Finally, the notion of enterprise competition—firms competing against each other—is described and explained in terms of analyzing competitors.

LEVELS OF MARKET COMPETITION

One way to delineate the set of competitors is to consider other products in terms of their proximity to the physical attributes of the brand. As Figure 2–2 shows, the problem of defining competition can be viewed as defining a set of concentric circles with the brand in question at the center.

The narrowest perspective one can take of competition is called *product form*. This reflects the view that the main competitors are those brands in the product category that are going after the same segment. As Figure 2–2 shows, from Diet Coke's perspective, a narrow view of competition would include only the diet colas such as Diet-Rite and Diet Pepsi. Similarly, although Packard Bell, IBM, and Apple all offered personal computers, only the latter two competed actively for the business market while the former concentrated on home users. Thus, product form competition is a narrow view of competition and focuses mainly on what competitors' current offerings are and not what could happen in the (possibly near) future.

The second level of competition is based on those products or services with similar features, a feature being defined as the presence of a characteristic (e.g., calories), not its value (e.g., high or low). This type of competition, called *product category*, is what managers typically think of as a definition for the competitive set. For example, all firms producing personal computers, regardless of the target market, are competitors. All soft drinks (see Figure 2–1) form a "market" as well. Firms specializing in the collection of retail sales data, such as A. C. Nielsen and IRI, define product categories or markets based on the similarity of physical attributes. While

FIGURE 2–2
Example of Levels of Competition

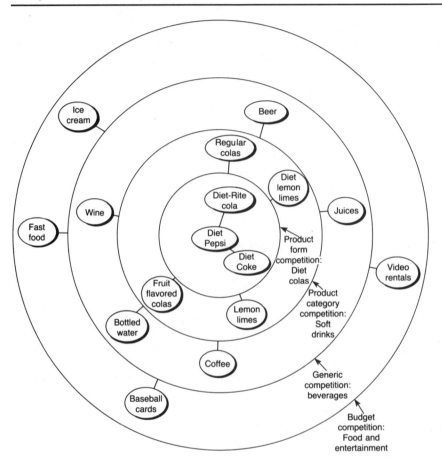

somewhat broader than product form competition, this product category definition of competition still takes a short-run view of the market definition problem.

The third level of competition is more long term in nature and focuses on substitutable product categories. Termed *generic competition* by Kotler (1988), it defines the competition and the market as consisting of those products or services fulfilling the same customer need. Thus, soft drinks compete with orange juice in the "thirst-quenching" market, fast-food outlets compete against frozen entrées in the "convenience" eating market, and so on.

This need-based perspective is essential if a manager wishes to avoid both overlooking threats and ignoring opportunities. This perspective is well described in Levitt's (1960) classic article that admonishes several industries for defining their businesses too narrowly. Railroads viewed themselves as providing rail-based rather than general transportation services and lost business to trucks and airlines. Steel companies thought they were providing steel rather than general structural material; automobile manufacturers wanted the latter so they substituted plastics in some areas of the cars. Some firms take this generic perspective. Federal Express, for example, saw its competitors as not only Purolator, UPS (United Parcel Service), and the U.S. Postal Service, but also other companies providing quick transmission of information. As a result, Federal Express tried to develop a facsimile business as an alternative to overnight package and letter delivery.

An even more general level of competition, termed *rivalry* by Kotler (1988), is *budget* competition. This is the broadest view of competition; it considers all products and services competing for the same customer dollar as forming a market. For example, a consumer who has $500 in discretionary disposable income could spend it on a vacation, a ring, a money market instrument, or a variety of other things. *The Wall Street Journal* (1986) noted that because of a healthy U.S. economy, people had been spending money on consumer durables rather than at fast-food chains such as Wendy's or McDonald's. Competition for dollars is even tighter when the economy is not so healthy, as the early 1990s have demonstrated. While a budget-level view of competition is conceptually useful, it is very difficult to implement strategically because it implies an enormous number of competitors.

Some examples should put the market definition problem in perspective. Consider the competition facing the marketing manager for a line of low-priced stereo components such as Pioneer. First, there are the competitors fighting for the same segment of the stereo market. Second, there are other, higher-priced component manufacturers. Third, manufacturers of other entertainment products such as television sets and videocassette recorders must be considered. Finally, alternative ways to spend the money, such as on a vacation, could be relevant. These different sets of competitors create multiple marketing tasks. First, the manager's brand must be shown to have advantages over competitors' brands in the low-price segment. Second, the advantages of the low-price components over more expensive ones (e.g., Bang and Olufsen, Macintosh) must be established. Third, the customers must be persuaded to buy stereos rather than, say, VCRs. Finally, the prospects have to be informed about the benefits of buying stereos instead of going on vacation or buying stocks. Thus, market definition has implications not only for defining the market but for the strategy employed as well.

FIGURE 2–3

Diet Pepsi Competitors

Level of Competition	Definition	Competing Company	Need Satisfied
Product form	Diet colas	Coca-Cola	Low-calorie, nonalcoholic, cola-flavored carbonated beverage
Product category	Soft drinks	Hicks & Haas (which now owns 7UP), Procter & Gamble	Nonalcoholic carbonated beverage
Generic	Food and beverages	Grand Metropolitan, PLC (Burger King), Seagrams (wine), Perrier (bottled water)	Food and drink
Budget	Food and entertainment	3M (VHS tapes), Topps (baseball cards)	Enjoyment

As a second example, consider the task facing the product manager for Diet Pepsi. Clearly it competes with other diet colas such as Diet Coke, but it also competes with other soft drinks, especially nondiet colas and diet lemon-limes. Further, it competes with most food and beverages (wines and bottled waters as a drink with a meal, ice creams as a treat, and so forth). Finally, to some extent, it competes with other low-ticket entertainment products such as baseball cards and video rentals. (See Figure 2–3 for one possible delineation of competitors based on this concept.)

A similar approach can be used to define competitors for Federal Express in the overnight package delivery market. Such a delineation might be that shown in Figure 2–4.

It is also important to note that, as one moves from product form toward budget competition, the customer targets also begin to change. Product form competition suggests battling for exactly the same customer in terms of who they are and why they buy. (But not necessarily where or when they buy: one soft drink manufacturer may concentrate on fountain sales—Coke—and another on grocery store sales—Pepsi.) As you move toward budget competition, both who they are and why they buy begin to differ as the need satisfied becomes more general. Since the key to a business is customers, this suggests that the most crucial form of competition will *generally* be product form, since they compete directly for the same customers. On the other hand, generic competition can destroy entire product categories when a major innovation occurs, and thus it, too, requires attention, especially for long-run planning.

FIGURE 2–4
Federal Express Competitors

Level of Competition	Definition	Companies	Need Satisfied
Product form	Overnight air delivery	Emery, Purolator	Exact form transmission of material overnight picked up and delivered
Product category	Small package delivery, facsimile	American Airlines, UPS, U.S. Post Office	Rapid transmission of exact form
Generic	Transportation and transmission of information	AT&T, IBM, MCI, Telex, Southwest Airlines (people movement)	Movement of parts and information
Budget	Provision of parts and information	Parts wholesalers and dealers, libraries	Provision of parts and information

Those products thought of as substitutes, and therefore competitors, may also be viewed as complements, such as soda and hamburgers. When viewed this way, potential competitors can be turned into allies in various joint ventures (e.g., cooperative advertising). Thus, this delineation of competitive levels defines potential competitors and not necessarily mortal foes.

Another valuable way to conceptualize the definition of competitors is to incorporate market segments into the model. Consider the market for travel services shown in Figure 2–5. We list the modes of travel on the left side of the figure. These are the generic competitors (i.e., they satisfy the benefit of providing transportation). Across the top, we list possible market segments. These could be defined in many ways, depending on the benefit being analyzed.

The figure has the following interpretation. One column of the figure is generic competitors for that segment. Consider the San Francisco to Los Angeles route. For the business traveler, the major competitors are airlines. However, for tourists, airlines, trains, car rental agencies, or driving your own car are substitutes. Students might consider buses and trains as the major competitors. Hence the level of competition across generic product forms/categories varies by customer segments.

In the short run, product form and product category competition are generally more critical. Consequently, most annual plans focus on these

FIGURE 2–5
Defining Competition Using Customer Segments

	Market Segments		
Generic Competitors	Business Travelers	Tourists	Students
Airlines	X	X	X
Bus		X	X
Train	X	X	X
Automobile (own)		X	X
Automobile (rent)		X	

almost exclusively. However, it seems foolish to not at least delineate more general forms of competition. Concentrating only on product form can allow a competitor to gain a massive share in a short time as a market shifts or a new technology appears (e.g., IBM's loss to Digital Equipment Company (DEC) in minicomputers and DEC's subsequent loss to Apple in microcomputers).

METHODS FOR DETERMINING COMPETITORS

The easiest way to define competition is to let someone else do it for you. Thus, the use of *existing categories* for frequently purchased goods or Standard Industrial Classification (SIC) codes for industrial products is popular and useful for uncovering exact form competition. The SIC system assigns products to two-digit major groups (e.g., 34, Fabricated Metal), three-digit groups (e.g., 342, Cutlery and Hand Tools), four-digit industries (e.g., 3423, Hand and Edge Tools), and five or more digit representations of products (e.g., 34231.11, Pliers). However, since these methods are generally based on either product form or product category, relying exclusively on these categories will overlook both generic and budget competitors.

Another way to define competitors is based on the *technical feasibility of substitution*. An engineering assessment suggests what other products could serve the same function as the one in question. This defines *potential competitors,* competitors whose products and customers may be worth considering targeting. However, this method does not explicitly consider customer perceptions and consequently would overlook competition between, say, ice cream and soda.

There are basically two more approaches to assessing the set of competitors facing a brand: managerial judgment and customer-based evaluation. We discuss them in detail next.

Managerial Judgment

Through experience, salesperson call reports, distributors, or other company sources, managers can often develop judgments about the sources of present and future competition.

One way to structure the thought process is through the use of tabular material such as that shown in Figure 2–6, a variant of Ansoff's (1965) well-known growth matrix. Box A represents product form competition; that is, those products or services that are basically the same and that are pursuing the same customers. Box C represents product form competitors that target other customers.

The most interesting cell in Figure 2–6 is B. This cell represents potential future competitors who already have a franchise with our customers but do not offer the same product or service. In this case, the manager might try to forecast which firms in B are likely to become more direct competitors. Examples of capitalization on prior customer familiarity with a company are numerous. If we consider telecommunications, IBM has a considerable franchise with large business customers through its mainframe computer business. IBM thus easily moved to cell A through its purchases of MCI and Rolm. If we consider the orange juice market, Procter & Gamble has perhaps the best franchise of any consumer products manufacturer with both supermarkets and consumers, which it used to develop the Citrus Hill brand of orange juice. This type of movement is common in retail businesses where companies often try to use their "brand franchise" in one category to grab sales in others that serve the same customers (e.g., Nike's unsuccessful move into clothing). Managers should assess the

FIGURE 2–6
Managerial Judgment of Competition

Markets	Product/Services	
	Same	Different
Same	A	B
Different	C	D

likelihood of such horizontal movements as well as their chances of success. (Interestingly, in 1992 P&G dropped out of the 100 percent fruit juice market, indicating its Citrus Hill brand was less than totally successful.)

Cell D competitors are very difficult to predict as they currently sell different products to different markets. One example of the impact of such a competitor was Litton Industries' commercialization of microwave technology in the area of consumer durables, which created a new competitor in the kitchen appliance market for General Electric.

One unscientific but useful way to see what a product or service might compete with is to imagine the item as a "prop" for a stand-up comedian. The comedian, unencumbered by convention (and sometimes good taste), can create many uses for a product, therefore suggesting different competitive products.

Customer-Purchase-Based Measures

Two types of customer data are commonly used to assess competitive market structures: actual purchase or usage data and judgments (Day, Shocker, and Srivastava, 1979). While the former represent actual behavior, they indicate only what customers actually have done and not what they would have preferred to do in the past or will do in the future. Thus, behavioral data are more useful for assessing current market structure than future structure.

Several measures of competition based on past behavior have been proposed: (1) brand switching, (2) interpurchase times, and (3) cross-elasticity of demand. We discuss these measures in detail.

Brand Switching

Probabilities of brand switching have been proposed as measures of customers' perceived similarities and, therefore, substitutability among brands (Kalwani and Morrison, 1977; Lehmann, 1972). High brand-switching probabilities thus imply a high degree of competition.

Consider the three cases represented in Figure 2–7. In the first case (I), repeat rates (brand loyalties) are between 60 and 75 percent, a fairly high level. When A is not repeat purchased, however, almost all past buyers of A switch to B (35(35 + 2 + 3) = 87.5%). Similarly, nonrepeaters of B switch to A (83.3%). By contrast, nonbuyers of C switch to D and nonbuyers of D switch to C (85.7 and 80 percent, respectively). This suggests close competition exists between brand pairs A and B and C and D. This often occurs because A and B share a common attribute (e.g., are both diet drinks).

By contrast, in case II in Figure 2–7, brand A has a higher repeat rate (90 percent) than any other brand, suggesting its customers are more satisfied and loyal. When customers switch from Brands B, C, and D, they tend

FIGURE 2–7
Brand-Switching Data

I. **Two Clear Submarkets**

		Brand Bought at Time t + 1			
		A	B	C	D
Brand Bought at Time t	A	.60	.35	.02	.03
	B	.25	.70	.03	.02
	C	.01	.04	.65	.30
	D	.03	.02	.20	.75

II. **A Dominant Brand**

		Brand Bought at Time t + 1			
		A	B	C	D
Brand Bought at Time t	A	.90	.03	.02	.05
	B	.40	.40	.10	.10
	C	.30	.05	.60	.05
	D	.40	.04	.06	.50

III. **All-Weak-Brands Market**

		Brand Bought at Time t + 1			
		A	B	C	D
Brand Bought at Time t	A	.40	.20	.18	.22
	B	.20	.35	.20	.25
	C	.27	.19	.30	.34
	D	.17	.18	.35	.30

to switch to brand A. Thus, brand A is clearly a strong brand. In some sense, brand A is a strong competitor for brand B, but brand B is not a strong competitor for brand A. This type of pattern tends to emerge when there is a clear leader (possibly a market pioneer) and a number of "me-too" brands that offer lower quality at periodically lower prices (i.e., on sale).

Finally, consider case III. Here the repeat rate is below 50 percent for all four brands and nonrepeat purchasers are likely to switch to any other brand. This suggests brands don't matter very much (i.e., have little equity), perhaps because customers simply pick either whatever brand an outlet carries or because they buy whatever is on promotion. There is one interesting result in case III: buyers of brand C are more likely to switch to brand D than repeat purchase and vice versa. This could be because brands C and D alternate their promotions (and customers buy on promotion), because brands C and D are complements rather than substitutes (competitors), or because multiple parties (e.g., family members) are making the purchases. In any event, in case III, all brands seem to compete with all others fairly equally.

As with any analysis of customers, when interpreting aggregate results, it is important to recognize that different customers may view a market quite differently. In case III in Figure 2–7, the apparently diffuse competition based on this aggregate switching data may mask clear markets (e.g., similar to cases I and II) that are "averaged out." While an aggregate view of competition is an important starting point, a revised, more focused view may be needed once attention turns to particular target segments.

A major drawback to brand-switching measures is that the brands must be specified a priori, which constrains the breadth of the competitive set of products. Brand-switching measures are usually most useful in determining competitors for frequently purchased goods or services. Another problem with these measures is that, as McAlister and Lattin (1985) argue, brand switches occur across complements as well as substitutes. Complements might be sought when consumers want variety. For example, a consumer may become bored with Coke and switch to 7UP. A researcher would only observe a brand switch from Coke to 7UP for that consumer. Depending on whether one attributed the switch to substitution or variety seeking, the revealed competitive structure might look quite different. Still another problem with using purchase data is that most sources of it, such as consumer panel data, are at the aggregate (household) level. Thus, switching between Diet Pepsi and Heineken might indicate whether the 13-year-old daughter or the father made the purchase and not that soda and beer compete. Therefore, using actual brand-switching data to define competition is useful but far from infallible.

Interpurchase Times
Using an interpurchase time criterion (Fraser and Bradford, 1983), two items are said to be perfect substitutes and, therefore, competitors if

$$E(X_{ii}) = E(X_{ij})$$

where $E(X_{ii})$ is the expected interpurchase interval for a repeat purchase of brand i, and $E(X_{ij})$ is the time interval between switching from i to j. Shocker, Zahorik, and Stewart (1984) evaluate this approach, which is useful only for frequently purchased items and is not widely used.

Cross-Elasticity of Demand
The cross-elasticity of demand is the percentage change in one brand's sales with respect to a percentage change in another brand's price (or other marketing variable). If a cross-elasticity with respect to price is positive (i.e., a

brand's sales decline when another brand's price drops), the two brands or products are considered to be competitive.

Several authors have used cross-elasticities to define markets (see Cooper, 1988). The major problem with this approach is the estimation of the cross-elasticities; it is generally assumed (1) there is no competitive reaction to the price cut, and (2) the market is static with respect to new entrants, product design, and so forth. As with brand-switching measures, the set of brands or products usually must be defined a priori.

In summary, the behavioral measures are useful in that they represent what customers actually do; they are not mere speculation. For the most part, however, they have been applied to frequently purchased, nondurable goods. (For an exception, see an analysis of the automobile market by McCarthy, Kannan, Chandrasekharan, and Wright, 1992). In addition, they tend to be most appropriate where a product class is defined a priori and what is being sought is a set of market definitions based on product form or category competition.

Customer-Judgment-Based Measures

Four judgmental measures have been proposed (Shocker, 1986): (1) overall similarity, (2) similarity of consideration sets, (3) product deletion, and (4) substitution in use. Although not based on actual customer behavior, they provide insight into potential future market structures, produce broader definitions of current structures, and are applicable to all types of products and services, including industrial products and consumer durables.

Overall Similarity

Judged similarity measures between products or brands can be used to create geometric representations in multidimensional spaces called *perceptual maps*. The brands or products are represented by points in the space, while the dimensions represent the attributes utilized by the customers in making the similarity judgments. Brands located close to each other are judged to be similar on the attributes and thus form a defined market.

For example, Figure 2–8 presents a perceptual map from the generic category of desserts. Although the analysis does (and must) begin with a prespecified set of alternatives, the set can be developed through focus group research emphasizing products satisfying a given need. The points not attached to the vectors represent the various dessert products. Information about the competitive sets is obtained by examining clusters of points. The upper-right quadrant would be very useful to, say, the General Foods brand manager for Jell-O. From the map, it is clear that Jell-O is

FIGURE 2–8

Defining Competition with Perceptual Mapping

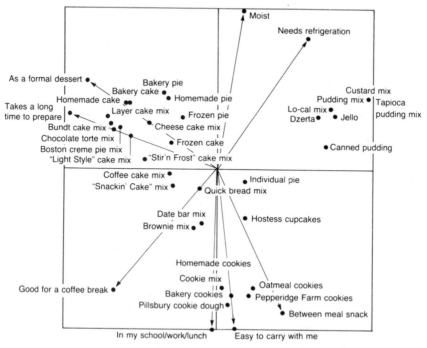

Source: *Marketing News,* May 14, 1982, p. 3.

perceived to be similar to custard, pudding, tapioca, Lo-Cal, and D-zerta. The vectors help to determine the attributes defining the space but are not relevant to the market structure issue.

Similarity of Consideration Sets

An approach developed by Bourgeois, Haines, and Sommers (1979) asks customers to take a large set of products and divide them into piles representing those that are thought to be substitutable, that is, that would be considered together on a purchase occasion. The customers are then asked to judge the similarity of the products within each pile. By accumulating similarity judgments across the customers, a perceptual map can be developed. Thus, this approach is somewhat similar to the preceding one but collects the similarity judgments after the formation of consideration sets. Other variants of this approach use verbal protocol data (customers thinking aloud as they consider a decision).

Product Deletion

Urban, Johnson, and Hauser (1984) developed a market definition based on customer reaction to product unavailability. A set of products or brands are presumed to be substitutes and consequently form a market if, when one of them is deleted from the choice set, customers are more likely to buy from the remaining products than from a set of products outside the original set.

For example, suppose a choice set for stereos consists of Pioneer, Sansui, and Technics. If, when Pioneer is eliminated from the set, customers are more likely to choose Sansui or Technics than Macintosh or any other brand, then the three brands are presumed to form a market.

Although described by authors as being primarily useful to partition product form markets into submarkets, the approach could be used in a more general setting. For example, a choice set could consist of milk, orange juice, and soft drinks. If milk were unavailable and the orange juice and soft drinks were subsequently chosen more often than tea or coffee, then milk, juice, and soft drinks apparently compete at the generic level.

Substitution in Use

Stefflre (1972) developed a procedure that has the potential to uncover broad generic market definitions. Customers are first given the target product or brand and asked to develop a list of all its possible uses. Next, they are asked to list other products or brands that provide the same uses or benefits. Since a large group of products results from these two steps, an independent sample of customers might be asked to rate the products on their appropriateness for the uses specified.

As an illustration, suppose the target product of interest is a checking account. A brief sketch of the analysis is provided below:

Checking Account Analysis

Use	Pay bills	Transactions	Security of money
Substitutes	Pay by phone	Credit cards	Traveler's checks
Competitors	AT&T	Visa	American Express

Thus, substitution in use can produce a set of fairly diverse competitors.

Summary

The methods for determining competition are summarized in Figure 2–9 along two dimensions: (1) the usefulness of each method for determining competition at a certain level, and (2) the kind of research data typically

FIGURE 2-9

Methods versus Competition Levels and Information Required*

Approach	Level of Competition				Typical Data Sources	
	Product Form	Product Category	Generic	Budget	Primary	Secondary
Existing definitions	X	X				X
Technical feasibility substitution	X				X	
Managerial judgment	X	X	X		X	X
Customer behavior based:						
Brand switching	X	X				X
Interpurchase times	X	X				X
Cross-elasticities	X	X	X			X
Customer evaluation based:						
Overall similarity	X	X	X		X	
Similarity of consideration sets	X	X	X	X	X	
Product deletion	X	X	X		X	
Substitution in use	X	X	X		X	

*An X indicates that either the method is useful for determining competition at that level or it employs data of a certain type.

used to implement the method. With respect to the latter, information is divided into primary sources (data collected specifically to determine competitors) and secondary sources (data collected for some general purpose other than to determine the structure of the market).

As Figure 2–9 shows, all the methods are useful for determining product form competition. Managerial judgment and behavior-based customer data are mainly useful for developing product form and product category markets. Customer information that is judgment based, however, can be used to assess generic competition as well. Since cross-elasticities, similarity measures, product deletion, and substitution in use either start with an a priori market definition (although possibly a very broad one) or are usage based, they cannot be used to define budget competition, that is, those products fighting for the same customer dollar. Since the consideration-set approach has no such restrictions, it can be used to assess budget competition.

With respect to data requirements, the judgment-based customer evaluations require primary data, while behavior-based methods can use secondary data. In particular, the latter methods often use consumer panel data, which are records of household purchasing from a variety of product categories. Consumer judgments might supplement purchase data with primary data, such as interviews focusing on motivations for brand switching. Managerial judgment can (and at least implicitly does) utilize both primary (e.g., interviews with distributors) and secondary (e.g., salesperson call reports) data.

COMPETITOR SELECTION

While examining competition at four levels makes sense intuitively, the practical implications for the market manager are substantial. As mentioned earlier, one implication is that marketing strategy must be developed with an eye toward four different problems: (1) convincing customers in your segment that your brand is best (product form competition); (2) convincing buyers that your product form is best (product category competition); (3) convincing buyers that your product category is best (generic competition); and (4) convincing buyers that the basic need your product fulfills is an important one. A manager must decide what percentage of his or her budget to expend on handling each problem.

A second implication of the four levels of competition is that a selective competitor focus must be chosen. A manager cannot focus either analysis or actual strategy on each possible competitor in the market, however it is defined, because of limited resources. For example, the Pioneer marketing manager described earlier has to select which competitor to focus on—other low-priced stereos, other stereos, or other entertainment forms.

Deciding which competitors to focus on can be facilitated by examining three factors: (1) the time horizon of marketing plan being developed (short versus long run), (2) the stage of the product life cycle relevant for the product, and (3) the rate of change in the technology.

In a one-year operating marketing plan, competition should be defined on both product form and product category bases as they reflect the short-term competitive outlook. For example, in the short run, Sanka's major competitors are primarily other decaffeinated instant coffees and secondarily other instant or regular coffees. On the other hand, for longer-term plans, all four levels of competition are relevant with special emphasis on the generic level to identify important competitive threats, especially from new technologies.

The stage in the product life cycle may be relevant to defining competition. At the early growth stages of a product, particularly a new technology, competition should be broadly (generically) defined since a large part of the marketing task is persuading customers to substitute a new product for an existing one that was satisfying the consumers' needs. On the other hand, in mature markets, the focus should generally be on product form and category competitors to best assess whether or not to stay in a market.

Finally, where the rate of technological change is rapid, competition should be conceived as broadly as possible. This is characteristic of the communications field as such diverse products as word processors, home computers, cable TV, and satellites compete for certain services. Alternatively, narrow definitions (i.e., product form) are sufficient where new technical advances occur less frequently, as with food products.

Given that the appropriate levels of competition have been selected (i.e., the market has been defined), attention shifts to choosing the relevant competitors on which to focus. This assessment requires an initial pass at competitor analysis. The factors determining which competitors are relevant are related to the forecasts of the brands' likely strategies, which are the major outputs of competitor analyses. However, the resources the competitors can bring to bear in the market are also critical. This focus on resources highlights a final perspective on competition called *enterprise competition*.

ENTERPRISE COMPETITION

Ultimately, brands do not compete against each other in a vacuum. The company's resources are a key determinant of its vulnerability to a marketing strategy. Thus, while we have examined competition in this chapter from the perspective of a brand or product, firm versus firm or enterprise competition involves selection of the competitors against which strategies are mounted.

As an illustration, consider the personal computer market. On a product form basis, Apple's Macintosh competes against IBM, Compaq, Tandy, Packard Bell, Dell, and Gateway, among others. However, it is clear that not all competitors are created equal. When Apple tries to go head to head with IBM in the business market, it competes not only in terms of product features against IBM's personal computers but also against IBM's resources in terms of dollars, sales force, image, and willingness to support its products.

It is often difficult to understand brand level competition without understanding the broader context in which it occurs. For example, it is hard to understand the BIC versus Cricket lighter battle without recognizing the general competition between BIC and Gillette, which includes razors and pens as well as lighters.

Enterprise competition is often characterized by asymmetries in competitive perspectives. For example, Hyundai undoubtedly views General Motors as a competitor, but the reverse is probably not true. This does not mean the two corporations' product lines do not overlap, but that from the enterprise perspective, GM views Ford, Chrysler, and Toyota as more potent adversaries and thus stronger threats to its competitive position.

SUMMARY

In this chapter, we argued that the set of competitors that pose a threat to a brand can be highly varied and come from a variety of industries. Therefore, a "market" is often dynamic and difficult to define. We presented a framework to conceptualize competition and methods to help form ideas about the competitive set. Finally, we discussed approaches to selecting competitors in terms of choosing the relevant levels and specific brands.

Essentially, we suggest competitors are those companies whose products or services compete for the same customer either directly through offering similar products or services (product form or category competition), indirectly through satisfying similar basic needs (generic competition), or in terms of budget. Clearly, one can develop an essentially infinite list of competitors. In general, for a short-run plan (say, one year) most of the effort should be directed toward exact-form and similar-form competitors with relatively little attention to products that will only gradually affect your sales (e.g., bottled water if you sell wine). The longer the range of the plan, the more attention should turn to less similar competitors, especially those who are strong and have or are developing technologies that could threaten your business (e.g., computers if you sell typewriters).

REFERENCES

Abell, Derek F. *Defining the Business.* Englewood Cliffs, N.J.: Prentice Hall, 1980.

Ansoff, H. Igor. *Corporate Strategy.* New York: McGraw-Hill, 1965.

Bourgeois, Jacques D.; George H. Haines; and Montrose S. Sommers. "Defining an Industry." Presented at the ORSA/TIMS Conference on Market Measurement, Stanford, Calif., 1979.

Cooper, Lee G. "Competitive Maps: The Structure Underlying Asymmetric Cross Elasticities." *Management Science* 34 (June 1988), pp. 707–23.

Day, George S.; Allan D. Shocker; and Rajendra K. Srivastava. "Customer-Oriented Approaches to Identifying Product Markets." *Journal of Marketing* 43 (Fall 1979), pp. 8–19.

"Fast-Food Slump Hits Industry Giants as More Competition Bites into Profit." *The Wall Street Journal,* April 22, 1986.

Fraser, Cynthia, and John W. Bradford. "Competitive Market Structure Analysis: Principal Partitioning of Revealed Substitutabilities." *Journal of Consumer Research* 10 (June 1983), pp. 15–30.

Kalwani, Manohar U., and Donald G. Morrison. "A Parsimonious Description of the Hendry System." *Management Science* 23 (January 1977), pp. 467–77.

Kotler, Philip. *Marketing Management,* 6th ed. Englewood Cliffs, N.J.: Prentice Hall, 1988.

Lehmann, Donald R. "Judged Similarity and Brand-Switching Data as Similarity Measures." *Journal of Marketing Research* 9 (August 1972), pp. 331–34.

Levitt, Theodore. "Marketing Myopia." *Harvard Business Review,* July–August 1960, pp. 45–56.

McAlister, Leigh, and James M. Lattin. "Using a Variety-Seeking Model to Identify Substitute and Complementary Relationships among Competing Products." *Journal of Marketing Research* 22 (August 1985), pp. 330–39.

McCarthy, Patrick S.; P. K. Kannan, Radha Chandrasekharan; and Gordon P. Wright. "Estimating Loyalty and Switching with an Application to the Automobile Market." *Management Science* 38 (October 1992), pp. 1371–93.

Shocker, Allan D. "A Bibliography of Recent Work in Market Definition and Structure." Working Paper, Owen Graduate School of Management, Vanderbilt University, 1986.

Shocker, Allan D.; Anthony J. Zahorik; and David W. Stewart. "Competitive Market Structure Analysis: A Comment on Problems." *Journal of Consumer Research* 11 (December 1984), pp. 836–41.

Stefflre, Volney. "Some Applications of Multidimensional Scaling to Social Science Problems." In *Multidimensional Scaling: Theory and Applications in the Behavioral Sciences,* vol. III. Ed. A. K. Romney, R. N. Shepard, and S. B. Nerlove. New York: Seminar Press, 1972.

Urban, Glen L.; Philip L. Johnson; and John R. Hauser. "Testing Competitive Market Structures." *Marketing Science* 3 (Spring 1984), pp. 83–112.

CHAPTER 3

INDUSTRY ANALYSIS

OVERVIEW

Analyzing a market's trends and attractiveness is important for several reasons. First, market (which we use synonymously with industry in this context) attractiveness determines whether current competitors are likely to continue in the market and whether others are likely to enter. While predicting the exact timing of a move is difficult, it was reasonable to expect GE to leave the consumer electronic and aerospace businesses (given its stated goal to be number 1 or 2, particularly in high-margin businesses) and for DEC to (belatedly) enter the microcomputer business. Hence industry attractiveness provides a focus on the future rather than simply current or past competitors. Second, the state of an industry (in terms of future profits and growth) often determines the level of commitment (both dollars and top human resources) devoted to it by competitors, a key part of competitive analysis, as well as reasonable levels to expect in terms of margins and profits. Third, analysis of key trends in technology, regulation, and so on suggests major threats and opportunities. Analyzing a market is crucial to developing sound objectives and strategies. This chapter, therefore, is devoted to assessing a market's present and future characteristics.

Industry or market attractiveness is so important that almost all strategic planning models utilize it at least partially. Whether approaching from a new or existing product perspective, an initial question asked before the planning process can begin is whether the industry is sufficiently attractive to warrant investment in it, either by your company, current competitors, or potential competitors. For example, the product portfolio of the Boston Consulting Group uses market growth rate as a proxy for attractiveness. Other models (Kerin, Mahajan, Varadarajan, 1990, chap. 3) utilize a two-dimensional strategic grid consisting of market attractiveness and business position.

A market is an evolving entity. Sometimes dramatic changes in technology or regulation reshape it almost overnight (e.g., the breakup of AT&T), but more typically a series of less powerful forces and events leads to a seemingly smooth and gradual evolution (as in the improvement in computer speed and power). What is needed is an assessment of the fundamentals of the industry being considered. Given that the industry has been defined (see Chapter 2), an essential component of the marketing planning process is an analysis of the potential for a firm to achieve a desired level of return on its investment.

The characteristics of an industry rarely all point in the same direction. As a result, markets that some firms find attractive will be of little interest to others. For example, most observers consider the luxury car market (over $30,000) to be overpopulated with models, particularly with the introduction of Toyota's Lexus and Nissan's Infiniti. In addition, European manufacturers are very sensitive to declines in the value of the dollar, which makes their cars very expensive in the important U.S. market. However, Ford recently purchased the British firm Jaguar because Ford felt that there is considerable brand equity in the name and the label would give the company an instant entry into the luxury car field. Similarly, the fast-food industry is considered to be mature in terms of sales growth, but new concepts such as drive-up-only hamburger stands have recently been introduced. General Electric obviously found household appliances (1984), consumer electronics (1989), and aerospace (1992) unattractive and sold those divisions. But the buyers—Black and Decker, Thompson, and Martin Marietta—obviously found the same markets attractive. (Interestingly, Thompson sold its medical products division to General Electric at the same time GE sold consumer electronics to Thompson; in effect, the two firms traded businesses.) Hence attractiveness involves both industry/market factors and company factors (capabilities, goals).

This chapter considers three major categories of variables (Figure 3–1). First, we focus on basic descriptive statistics of the industry: its size and sales patterns. Next, we discuss several important aspects of the competitive and profit situation. Third, we discuss general environmental influences (technology, etc.). For each of these factors, the procedure has two important steps. First, past and current data are gathered and interpreted. That is, analysis goes beyond mere listing of facts. Then, projections are made. For example, current margins may be 20 percent. A key issue, however, is what margins will be in two years. These projections are important because they affect other analyses (i.e., if new competitors are expected, then they must be analyzed in the subsequent competitive analysis section) and provide many of the basic planning assumptions behind forecasts and profit projections.

FIGURE 3–1
Bases for Industry Analysis

Market Factors
  Size
  Growth
  Stage in life cycle
  Cyclicity
  Seasonality
  Marketing mix
  Profits
  Financial ratios
Competitive Factors
  Concentration
  Power of buyers
  Power of suppliers
  Rivalry
  Pressure from substitutes
  Capacity utilization
  Entries and exits
Environmental Factors
  Technological
  Economic
  Social
  Political
  Regulatory

AGGREGATE MARKET FACTORS

Size

Market size (measured in both units and dollars) is clearly an important criterion as it relates to the likelihood of a product obtaining revenues to support a given investment. Large markets also offer more opportunities for segmentation than small ones (see Chapter 5). Therefore, both large firms and entrepreneurial organizations might find large markets attractive. Large markets, however, tend to draw competitors with considerable resources, often making such markets unattractive for small firms, as in the soft drink industry. Thus, absolute size is not by itself sufficient to warrant new or continuing investment.

In describing the size of a market, it is also useful to describe the size of its major subunits. For example, the soft drink market divides into subcategories based on calories (diet versus nondiet), flavor (cola, lemon-lime, etc.), and whether real juice is included. In addition, various markets that compete with the soft drink category, such as bottled water and fruit juice, also should be tracked. This provides information and a focus on the impact of substitutes (generic competition) on the product category.

Growth

Not only is current growth important, but, because of the product life cycle, growth projections over the horizon of the plan are also critical. Fast-growing markets are almost universally desired because they support high margins and sustain profits into future years. However, they also attract competitors. For example, while Sony developed the U.S. market for video-cassette recorders, the projected high market growth rate supported the entry of other firms' marketing systems with a competing recording format (VHS), which now dominates Sony's Beta format.

A major factor relating to an industry is the rate at which products become obsolete (i.e., are replaced by new products). Whether product replacement is attractive or not depends heavily on a company's ability to design and market new products of good quality in a short time.

Life Cycle Stage

These two factors, market size and growth, are often portrayed simultaneously in the form of the product life cycle. This curve breaks down the sales of a product into four segments: introduction, growth, maturity, and decline. The introduction and growth phases are the early phases of the life cycle while sales are still growing, maturity represents a leveling off in sales, while the decline phase represents the end of the life cycle.

The attractiveness of products in each of the life cycle phases is not always clear. Products in the growth phase, such as personal computers in the 1980s, are generally thought to be attractive. However, as Osborne, Commodore, and others have found, high rates of market growth do not ensure success. Although mature markets are often disdained, clever marketers often find new ways to segment them, which creates opportunities. Witness the success of Reebok in the leisure footwear market and Miller's Lite beer. Finally, brands in declining product categories are also in an unfavorable position within the corporation, even though Harrigan (1980) gives several examples of strategies to turn these businesses around.

Cyclicity

Since many firms attempt to develop products and acquire entire companies to eliminate interyear sales cyclicity, this is not an attractive characteristic of an industry unless it balances out cycles in other components of a firm's business. Capital-intensive business, such as automobiles, steel, and chemicals, are often dependent on general business conditions and therefore suffer through peaks and valleys of sales as GNP and/or interest rates vary.

Seasonality

As with sales cyclicity, seasonality, or intrayear cycles in sales, is generally not viewed positively. Most industries are seasonal to some extent (e.g., ice cream, beer, travel services), but some are extremely so. The toy industry has tried to reduce its reliance on the Christmas period to generate most of its sales, and ski resorts have been promoted as four-season vacation destinations. Such seasonal business tends to generate price wars since there may be little other chance to obtain sales revenues.

Marketing Mix

The general trends in *distribution, pricing,* and *promotion* provide useful background for competitive and customer analysis as well as strategy formulation. For example, the recent trend toward direct marketing of PCs has major implications for the computer market. Similarly, the attempt by P&G to decrease trade promotion and use an "everyday low pricing" approach could smooth sales, thus improving production efficiency and increasing profits. Also, the use of "no-haggle" car pricing by Ford and others in 1992 could be an important trend or a short-run fad.

Profits

While there is certainly variability in profits, margins, and cash flows across products in an industry, there are also interindustry differences. For example, the profit margins for the soft drink, drug, machine tool, and tire industries in 1985 were 15.1 percent, 22.7 percent, 6.6 percent, and 7.6 percent, respectively (Standard & Poor's *Analyst Handbook,* 1986).

These differences in profitability are based on a variety of underlying factors. Differences can be due to factors of production (labor versus capital intensity, raw materials), manufacturing technology, and competitive rivalry, to name a few. Suffice it to say the industries that are chronically low in profitability are less attractive than those that offer higher returns.

A second aspect of profitability to consider is their variability over time. Variance in profitability is often used as a measure of industry risk. Semiconductors offer abnormally high return when demand is good but poor returns when demand slumps. Food-related businesses, on the other hand, produce steady if unspectacular profits. As is usually the case, there is a risk-return trade-off that must be made where the expected returns are evaluated against the variability in those returns.

Performance Ratios

Like profits, financial ratios vary substantially across competitors in an industry and hence are considered separately in a competitive analysis. Still there are substantial interindustry differences as well (see, for example, *Forbes* Annual Review). Most ratios are of the form return on _____; return on assets (ROA), return on equity (ROE), return on capital (ROC), and return on annual marketing expenditures. These ratios indicate both the rewards of successful performance and the requirements (e.g., capital intensity) for participation.

COMPETITIVE FACTORS

This section includes factors used by economists (Porter, 1980) to analyze an industry (the power of buyers and suppliers, competitive rivalry/pressure, and the pressure from substitutes), plus industry concentration and the threat of entries and exits.

Concentration

A simple indicator of the competition in an industry is its concentration, or the market share controlled by a few top firms. Various simple measures are used, such as:

1. The share of the largest firm.
2. The combined shares of the largest three or four firms.
3. The number of firms with at least X percent of the market (e.g., 1 percent).
4. The share of the largest firm divided by the share of the next three largest competitors.

A slightly more complex measure is the Herfindahl Index—the sum of the squared shares of the firms in the industry. This index goes from a high of 1 (when one firm has 100 percent share) to close to zero (when there are many firms with similar, small shares). In general, the more competitive the industry, the greater the requirements for marketing expenditures and the lower the profits.

Power of Buyers

Buyers are any people or institutions who receive finished goods or a service. These could be distributors, original equipment manufacturers (OEMs), retail stores, or end customers. Suppliers are any institutions that supply the industry with factors of production, such as labor, capital, and machinery.

High buyer bargaining power is negatively related to industry attractiveness. In such circumstances, buyers can force down prices and play competitors against each other for other benefits, such as service. Some conditions when buyer bargaining power is high include:

When the buyer accounts for a large percentage of the industry's output. The more important a buyer is to an industry's well-being (i.e., in terms of sales and profits), the more power the buyer has.

When the product is undifferentiated. If the industry views what it sells as a commodity, buyers will have a great deal of power. A good example of this is the leverage held by customers of commodity chemicals.

When the buyers are earning low profits. Ailing industries such as farm equipment can extract better terms from supplier industries than can healthy industries such as food processing.

When there is a threat by the buyer to backward integrate. Among other pressures felt by semiconductor manufacturers is the constant threat by computer manufacturers to make their own chips. IBM's purchase of part of Intel is such an example. Consumers also "backward integrate" as the growth of do-it-yourself hardware stores indicates.

When the buyer has full information. Consumers can exert more power in retail stores if they are fully aware of competitive offerings. For example, car dealers may be more willing to negotiate on price if the buyer signals that he or she is knowledgeable.

In general, consumers are limited in their buyer power on an individual basis. (Notable exceptions exist, such as the U.S. government as a purchaser of military equipment.) However, if consumers can be motivated as a group, they become a more important customer and thus exert more power than would otherwise be the case. For example, the highly desired dual-income couples in their 30s are considered to have large power since they are consumption oriented and may thus constitute a large portion of a seller's sales. Similarly, buying cooperatives have increased power.

Power of Suppliers

This is really just the mirror image of the buyer power assessment. High supplier power is clearly not an attractive situation as it allows suppliers to dictate price and other terms such as delivery dates to the buying industry. Some conditions when supplier bargaining power will be high are:

When suppliers are highly concentrated, that is, they are dominated by a few firms. Industries in need of supercomputers face strong suppliers since there are very few in the world.

When there is no substitute for the product supplied. The supercomputer falls into this category as well. By contrast, the power of the Organization of Petroleum Exporting Countries (OPEC) diminished as many industries converted plants to use both oil and coal.

When the supplier has differentiated its product and/or built in switching costs. Armco Inc. increased its power with the automobile industry by offering General Motors a delayed payment plan for its steel, a guarantee of no work stoppages, a demonstration of how cheaper steel could be substituted in certain areas, and extra service by supplying steel already prepared with adhesives. Sole-source suppliers have more power than multiple-source ones.

Rivalry

Industries characterized by intensive combat between the major participants may not be as attractive as those where the rivalry is more sedate. Often, a high degree of rivalry results in escalated marketing expenditures, price wars, employee raids, and other related activities. Such actions can go beyond what is considered to be "normal" market competition and can result in decreased welfare for both consumers and competitors.

Several examples highlight the negative aspects of rivalry. In the fast-food industry, Burger King and McDonald's periodically replay their "Battle of the Burgers." Advertising expenditures are increased, promotions and contests are run, but market shares change little; only profits are affected—usually negatively. A similar scenario exists in airline battles with frequent flier and other promotions. Several years ago, American offered triple mileage credit for program members; this was quickly copied by other airlines. Recently, other similar promotions such as "fly 3—get one free" have been introduced and then offered almost immediately by competitors. The result has been major losses for all airlines and the bankruptcy of several (Pan Am, Eastern, TWA, Continental, America West).

Some of the major characteristics of industries exhibiting intensive rivalry are summarized below:

Many or balanced competitors. The fast-food, automobile, and soft drink industries each have several large, well-endowed competitors. The personal computer market, once dominated by IBM, has recently become more competitive.

Slow growth. Again, fast food, autos, and soft drinks qualify. The relevant issue here is that in mature markets, growth can come only from another competitor.

High fixed costs. In such industries, there is extreme pressure to keep operations running at full capacity to keep average unit costs down. For this reason, capital-intensive industries such as paper and chemicals are highly competitive.

Lack of product differentiation. Basic commodities, such as aluminum, cattle, and chemicals, suffer from this problem, as do consumer products such as air travel. Any industry where the basic competitive weapon is price probably suffers from a lack of differentiation and its concomitant extensive rivalry.

Pressure from Substitutes

Substitutes are mainly generic or, to a lesser extent, budget competitors (see Chapter 2). Industries making products or delivering services for which there are a large number of substitutes are less attractive than those delivering a relatively proprietary service. Since almost all industries suffer from the availability of substitutes, this may not be a determining characteristic of an unattractive industry. However, some of the highest rates of return are earned by industries in which the range of substitutes is low. For example, as mentioned earlier, the drug industry, in which few legal substitutes are available, earns a high profit margin.

Capacity Utilization

A final characteristic to observe is the historical supply and demand situation in the industry. Chronic overcapacity is not a positive sign for long-term profitability. When an industry is operating at capacity, its costs stay low and its bargaining power with buyers is normally high. Thus, often a key indicator of the health of an industry is whether there is a consistent tendency toward operating at or under capacity.

Related to capacity utilization is the ease or difficulty of either adding new capacity or retiring unused capacity. This is typically assessed in terms of financial resources and time required. The trend toward outsourcing, using suppliers rather than producing parts inside the firm, is a way to gain more capacity flexibility. Hence, many firms' capacity depends heavily on their network of suppliers' capabilities.

Ease of Entries and Exits

One of the most important aspects of an industry has to do with its competitive structure, specifically the identity of competitors. As mentioned earlier, the same industry may be attractive for one company and unattractive for another. Nonetheless, a general pattern of characteristics tends to make them attractive. Basically, an industry tends to be attractive when it is large, growing, profitable, and noncompetitive, as Figure 3–2 indicates. It is important to analyze the likelihood of entrants and exits from a market and, if possible, their identity.

A high threat of new entrants diminishes the attractiveness of the industry. Except for the early stages of market development when new entrants can help a market expand, new entrants bring additional capacity and resources that usually heighten the competitiveness of a market and diminish margins. Even at early stages of market growth, the enthusiasm with which new entrants are greeted is tempered by who the competitor is. For example, while Apple publicly welcomed IBM's entry into the personal

FIGURE 3–2
Attractiveness to Entrants

	Attractiveness	
	High	*Low*
Market Factors		
Size	Large	Small
Growth	High	Slow
Stage in life cycle	Early	Late
Cyclicity	Low	High
Seasonality	Low	High
Marketing mix	?	?
Profits	High	Low
Financial ratios	High	Low
Competitive Factors		
Concentration	Low	High
Power of buyers	Low	High
Power of suppliers	Low	High
Rivalry	Low	High
Pressure from substitutes	Low	High
Capacity utilization	High	Low
Threat of entry	Low	High

computer market, it is unlikely there was continued private elation in Cupertino, California.

Key to the likelihood of new competitors entering a market are the barriers to entry that have been erected by the competition. Often these barriers are legal, such as those based on legislated monopolies (e.g., utilities) or on patents. But these barriers can change over time. When Xerox's patent on its basic copying process expired, the number of competitors in the copier market expanded dramatically. Besides formal barriers to entry or exit, other influences on entry/exit decisions include:

Economies of Scale.   An important barrier to entry into the automobile industry is the large plant size needed to operate efficiently, obtain quantity discounts on raw materials, and so on. Small manufacturers, such as Ferrari, must be content with serving the high-priced market segment. Areas other than manufacturing can obtain economies of scale. For example, hospital supply margins are better if many products are distributed simultaneously since order-taking costs are largely fixed.

Product Differentiation.   Well-established brand names and/or company reputations can make it difficult for new competitors to enter a market. In the ready-to-eat breakfast cereal industry, the big four—Kellogg Co., General Foods, General Mills, and Quaker Oats—have such long-established reputations that a new competitor would find it difficult to establish a brand franchise.

Capital Requirements.   These requirements could be related to both manufacturing facilities and marketing. For example, a major use of capital in the fast-food industry is for advertising and sales promotion. Most of the capital expenditures required to enter the farm equipment industry is for manufacturing facilities.

Switching Costs.   These are costs to buyers of switching from one supplier to another. If switching costs are high, such as they are in the mainframe computer business, it is difficult to convert a competitor's existing customers to you. For example, in 1974, American Hospital Supply (AHS) installed order-taking terminals in the stockrooms of large hospitals. This created a barrier to potential new entrants as hospitals routinely ordered AHS supplies through its proprietary system.

Distribution.   Shelf space can be difficult for new products to obtain. The splitting of Coke into Classic and New Coke, Coca-Cola's introduction of Diet Coke and Cherry Coke, and similar brand extensions by major competitor Pepsi have increased the pressure on competitors such as Seven-Up since this barrier to entry has been raised even higher. Recent attempts by supermarkets to obtain "slotting allowances," charges to manufacturers for placing goods on shelves, is a related barrier to entry, particularly for small firms. Similarly, some have argued that United's and American's airline reservation services provide an unfair advantage to those airlines.

The industry's willingness to vigorously retaliate against newcomers can also act as a barrier. When small Minnetonka Inc. introduced a pump dispenser for hand soap, both Colgate and Procter & Gamble immediately copied the package and outspent Minnetonka in promotion. That story has been replayed in numerous other industries.

ENVIRONMENTAL FACTORS

The environment includes those factors outside the control of both the firm and its industry. High susceptibility to changes in the environment is generally undesirable. As mentioned earlier in this chapter, if an industry's sales are tied to the domestic economic situation, cyclicity can result. Industries that are well positioned to take advantage of environmental changes may prosper.

Environmental factors can be put into five groups: technological, social, political, economic, and regulatory. These factors should be examined not only to assess industry attractiveness but also to determine if any forecasted changes in these areas dictate changes of strategy.

Technological

Technology refers to the procedures used for developing, making, and distributing a product or service to its customers (Capon and Glazer, 1987). In the narrowest sense, technology refers to the state of the art for *product design* (e.g., memory chips based on silicon) as well as the *production process* (i.e., hand versus automated assembly). A key issue, therefore, is whether any technologies are emerging that can affect or replace current industry technology.

Technological obsolescence is a major factor in many industries. Gradual obsolescence occurs as capabilities are upgraded (as in microprocessors, which went from 8086 to 286 to 386 to 486, each successive generation providing more speed and power). More discrete changes periodically occur in fabrics (e.g., nylon, Dacron, Gore-tex) and in document production (mechanical to electro-mechanical to electronic typewriters to PC-based word processing). Monitoring both continuous improvements and possible discrete changes is extremely important.

Major changes are occurring in the energy, materials, transportation, information, and genetic (bioengineering) areas. In information, for example, scanning systems at the cash registers in supermarkets enable retailers to monitor sales of different items for both inventory and shelf-space allocation decisions. Bioengineering research is being used to both improve crop yields and find cures for various diseases, including cancer.

Less technologically strong industries are particularly vulnerable to competition both from new industries and from foreign competitors that have invested in technology. Most major U.S. steel firms still used the blast furnace technology developed in the 1800s in the 1980s. Foreign steel firms and those domestic companies that invested in modern manufacturing technology have been highly successful in the past decade.

There is, however, a point beyond which technology can create a backlash, particularly among consumers. Naisbitt (1984) refers to this as "high tech versus high touch." For example, automatic teller machines have depersonalized banking to the point where some consumers yearn for the human contact afforded by tellers. Several years ago, Citibank in New York proposed allowing only its wealthiest customers to have personal contact for most transactions while others were forced to use machines. Consumers protested so vehemently that Citibank scrapped the idea.

Economic

Almost all capital goods industries (machine tools, computers) are sensitive to *interest rate fluctuations* since their high costs to buyers are often financed at short-term rates. Consumer durables such as homes, cars, and stereos are also sensitive to interest rates, although consumer credit rates do not react as much to changes in the prime lending rate as do commercial rates. Inflation rates are tied in with interest rate fluctuations and have a similar impact. Also, the impact of having foreign markets or producing in other countries can vary widely over time depending on *currency exchange rates*.

Since service businesses often hire relatively unskilled labor at low wage rates, they are highly dependent on *employment conditions*. When employment rates are high, for example, fast-food employees are hard to find as higher-paying jobs are available. The conditions of demand and supply of labor for each industry must be considered as well. The supply of engineers is cyclical. When supply is down, many firms in technically related businesses suffer from a shortage of skilled labor.

Industries that have broad customer bases (machine tools, copiers) are often sensitive to *fluctuations in GNP growth*. When the country is in a recession, so are these industries. This cyclicity is not an attractive feature of an industry.

Social

Trends in demographics, lifestyles, attitudes, and personal values among the general population are of particular concern for consumer products manufacturers for several reasons. First, new products have been developed to fit into today's lifestyles. Frozen entrées, for example, were developed to suit dual-career households with a need for convenience and easy preparation at dinnertime. Second, new features have been added to existing products. More upper-income households have ice water dispensers in refrigerators, fancy stereos in cars, and telephones with a memory for frequently called numbers. Finally, promotion has changed as well. How often do we see the aging "yuppie" on television ads?

Understanding lifestyle trends is also important for industrial product industries. Since the demand for industrial products is often derived demand (i.e., generated ultimately by consumers), changes in the source of that demand can affect demand for the end product. For example, when car demand slumps, so does the demand for steel, plastic, aluminum, and other industries heavily dependent on the auto industry.

For industrial companies, the key question to ask is whether the customers of the market being considered are in the "right" industries. Clearly, firms supplying the "hot" industries will do well, while those that are heavily tied to declining consumer products will not.

For consumer businesses, a key question to ask is whether the industry is positioned to take advantage of current trends. Some product areas that are "hot" because they appeal to baby boomers are furniture and electronic appliances, upscale fast-food chains, clothing, financial and travel services, and upscale baby accessories. Other products have been developed for consumers on the older edge of the baby boom generation. For example, a large part of the market for the Mazda Miata and other recently introduced convertibles are people over 40. Industries in trouble include colleges, coffee, cigarettes, and brown alcohol because they are being buffeted by either demographic or taste trends.

Political

An important environmental consideration is the industry's sensitivity to political factors. These are particularly relevant for products that have substantial foreign markets. Figure 3–3 conceptualizes the sources of political

FIGURE 3–3
Conceptualizing Political Risks

Sources of Political Risk	Groups through Which Political Risk Can Be Generated	Effects on International Business Operations
Competing political philosophies (nationalism, socialism, communism)	Government in power and its operating agencies	Confiscation: loss of assets without compensation
Social unrest and disorder	Parliamentary opposition groups	Expropriation with compensation: loss of freedom to operate
Vested interests of local business groups	Nonparliamentary opposition groups (Algerian "FLN," guerilla movements working within or outside country)	Operational restrictions: market shares, product characteristics, employment policies, locally shared ownership, and so on
Recent and impending political independence		
Armed conflicts and internal rebellions for political power	Nonorganized common interest groups: students, workers, peasants, minorities, and so on	Loss of transfer freedom: financial (dividends, interest payments, goods, personnel, or ownership rights, for example)
New international alliances	Foreign governments or intergovernmental agencies such as the EEC	
	Foreign governments willing to enter into armed conflict or to support internal rebellion	Breaches or unilateral revisions in contracts and agreements
		Discrimination such as taxes or compulsory subcontractings
		Damage to property or personnel from riots, insurrections, revolutions, and wars

Source: Stefan H. Robock, "Political Risk: Identification and Assessment." *Columbia Journal of World Business,* July–August 1971, p. 7. Copyright 1971. Reprinted with permission.

risk, the groups through which political risk can be generated, and the political problems' effect on the operation of the business.

For example, one of IBM's markets is South Africa. Following Figure 3–3, the sources of political risk are both social unrest and disorder and internal struggles for power. The groups responsible for the risk are largely nonorganized common interest groups. One effect on IBM's business could be possible damage to property and personnel from riots. However, another impact (not listed in Figure 3–3) is the potential loss of goodwill from people who resent IBM's presence in South Africa.

While such an analysis does not imply that a whole business is unattractive, it aids in the evaluation of geographically defined market segments. In addition, having a high percentage of sales come from risky foreign markets could lessen the industry's desirability.

Domestic U.S. political risk is generally not so great, but it is still important. It is usually related to which political party is in power. Republicans tend to favor free market economies. Therefore, industries pressed by foreign competition (e.g., shoes, textiles) would probably not receive any relief through quotas or tariffs. Democrats, tending to support some market intervention, might favor not only some of the above programs but also an industrial policy that would benefit certain industries. Defense spending and, hence, the fortunes of defense-related industries also have this type of political risk, as has been quite apparent recently.

Regulatory

Government and other agencies affect industry attractiveness through regulations. Some industries have become less attractive over time because laws have restricted their abilities to market or raise the overall cost of doing business. The cigarette industry, for example, has had restrictions placed on which media can be used for advertising. The mining, steel, and auto industries have all been affected by environmental and safety laws.

Summary

In this section, we identified major factors in the environment related to industry attractiveness. While each major factor is too complex to conveniently summarize here, it is clear that important influences on the long-term prospects for an industry lie outside its control.

While we have emphasized using environmental data to assess an industry's future health, it also can and should be used to plan new products and product improvements and select market segments.

DATA COLLECTION

Data collection is a vital part of an industry analysis. The aggregate market factors are pieces of information all firms should have regarding their businesses. The competitive factors are more qualitative, except for the capacity data. Most of these can be obtained through observing the relevant markets or speaking with industry participants. For example, the extent of industry rivalry is easily observed through the actions of the firms. Both market and competitive factors are easily obtainable from standard industry sources.

The environmental data present a different case. Many trends in the environment are not readily available from industry sources since trend spotting involves both data collection and analysis. One approach is to hire a professional trend spotter. Several firms specialize in collecting and analyzing environmental data. These include the Naisbitt Group (Washington, D.C.), Inferential Focus (New York), SRI International (Menlo Park, California), Yankelovich, Clancy, Schulman (Westport, Connecticut), Institute for the Future (Menlo Park, California), Langer Associates (New York), Brain Reserve (New York), Trend Union (Paris, New York), and Weiner Edrich Brown (New York). For fees ranging from $10,000 to $30,000 per year, these firms provide reports and personal consultations.

The alternative to hiring a consultant is to design an environmental scanning function within the company. A committee composed of managers representing different functional areas of the firm can replicate the activities of the consulting firms. The consultants generally are voracious consumers of printed media. Popular resources are national and regional newspapers, journals reporting new scientific developments (*Psychology Today, Scientific American*), "fringe" literature (*Mother Earth News, Heavy Metal*), and trend-tracking publications (*The Futurist, World Future Society Bulletin*). Environmental analysis depends on collecting information from as disparate sources as possible. The committee would be charged with clipping and abstracting relevant items, summarizing the data into a small number of key issues, and recommending strategies to deal with the issues.

Example

We offer two condensed illustrations of the preceding discussion. The information presented is meant to illustrate what could be done in assessing the attractiveness of an industry and is not necessarily complete.

Figure 3–4 was developed from research obtained on the bottled water market in 1989. There are many competitors in this market, with the total market composed of four product segments: domestic nonsparkling (leading brands: Sparkletts, Arrowhead), domestic sparkling (Arrowhead, Kentwood), imports (Perrier, Evian), and seltzers (Canada Dry, Schweppes).

In terms of aggregate market factors, the market is fairly attractive. This explains why many competitors have entered the business. It was a profitable market with good growth potential and no seasonality or cyclicity problems.

From the industry factors, the picture is more mixed. There are limited barriers to entry, which makes it relatively easy for new competitors to enter, particularly those already in a beverage-related business. The brands are relatively undifferentiated, with the chief exceptions being Perrier and

FIGURE 3–4
Industry Summary: Bottled Water Market (1989)

Aggregate Market Factors
1. Market size: $2.17 billion
2. Market growth: 10 percent average (1987–1992, projected)
3. Product life cycle: Late growth
4. Sales cyclicity: Negligible
5. Seasonality: Not significant
6. Profits: High

Industry Factors
1. Bargaining power of buyers: High
   Undifferentiated product
   Limited shelf space (retailers)
2. Bargaining power of suppliers: Negligible
   Most companies own their own water sources
3. Industry rivalry: High
   Many competitors (over 100 imported brands)
4. Pressure from substitutes: High
   Many other beverages
5. Industry capacity situation: Unknown
6. Threat of new entrants: High
   Limited barriers:
      Technology
      Limited natural water sources
      Distribution

Environmental Factors
1. Technological: Favorable
   Companies seeking competitive edge are adding flavors,
      changing packaging
2. Economic: Negligible
3. Social: Favorable
   Increased number of high-income people
   Social focus on health
4. Regulatory: Some
   Health standards
   Product definitions ("mineral" water)
5. Political: Negligible

Evian in the imported product segment, which gives consumers more reason to switch brands due to price. Also, competition is fairly intense. On the positive side, there are few problems with supply.

The environmental factors are also positive, particularly the social factors. Rising incomes and the increasing popularity of healthy, pure foods help bottled water sales. Most of the other factors are less important.

Selecting a significantly different product, Figure 3–5 was developed from research obtained on the technical workstation market in 1989. We define the product as single-user computers typically used by engineers and scientists that have superior computational power and graphics

FIGURE 3–5
Industry Summary: Technical Workstations (1989)

Aggregate Market Factors
 1. Market size: $4.1 billion in 1988
 2. Market growth: Expected to grow between 50% and 65% in 1989
 3. Product life cycle: Shortening
 4. Sales cyclicity: Negligible
 5. Seasonality: Negligible
 6. Profits: High; EBIT of 10% to 13%
Industry Factors
 1. Bargaining power of buyers: Moderate
     Growing number of suppliers
     Similar features offered
     But some product differentiation
 2. Bargaining power of suppliers: High
     Few firms are vertically integrated
     Japanese firms supply many chips and may give priority to Japanese firms
 3. Current industry rivalry: Moderate to high and increasing
     All large computer manufacturers are becoming committed to the market
 4. Pressure from substitutes: Exists but is not high
     Mini- and mainframe computers are being threatened by networked workstations
     High-end PCs are approaching older generation workstation computers.
 5. Industry capacity: Unknown but believed to be above 90% utilization
 6. Barriers to entry:
     Distribution
     Economies of scale
     Complementary assets
     High capital requirements
 7. Threat of new entrants: Very high
Environmental Factors
 1. Technological:
     Advances in microprocessor designs are a driving force in market
     Advances in PLDs and other semiconductors that reduce chip count result in lower
       prices
     Advances in technology are driving down price
     Operating software and application program innovations is the most significant driver
       in the marketplace
 2. Economic: No economic situations have affected the industry
 3. Social: Computer phobia is subsiding and computers are getting easier to use
 4. Regulatory: Negligible except for political risk
 5. Political: Significant political risk exists because of U.S./Japan trade relation tensions

capabilities. Computer vendors have developed products that are 8 to 40 times more powerful than personal computers and often more powerful than minicomputers. The major competitors are SUN Microsystems, Digital Equipment Corporation, IBM, and Hewlett-Packard through its acquisition of Apollo.

The aggregate factors paint a somewhat more attractive picture of this market compared to the bottled water market. The market is much bigger and growing. A significant factor in markets such as this is the quick pace of movement through the product life cycle.

The industry factors are more negative. First, the threat of new entrants is very high as any company with chipmaking or related technology can enter this market. For example, Intel, a large semiconductor manufacturer, decided to forward integrate into workstation manufacturing. With this increased competition, rivalry is increasing and buyers have more choices, which gives them more power. Also, the companies that buy chips from other firms could have supply problems in tight semiconductor markets.

A positive note is the set of environmental factors. Computers are becoming easier to use, thus lending themselves to a wider customer base. Technological advances result in lower prices from more efficient hardware design and greater ease of use from software improvements. Both of these factors are likely to greatly expand the market for technical workstations in the near future. Some mildly negative environmental aspects are the possible future relationship of workstation purchases to business cycles (economic factors) and potential trade tensions with Japan and Europe (political factors).

SUMMARY

This chapter has presented a framework for analyzing an industry. The three major sets of factors to consider are market factors, such as market size and growth; competitive factors, such as power of buyers and suppliers; and environmental factors, such as demographic and regulatory trends. Data can be assembled from a variety of sources. The most useful include trade associations, government publications, general business publications (*Forbes, Fortune, Business Week*), and company sources such as annual reports.

REFERENCES

Capon, Noel, and Rashi Glazer. "Marketing and Technology: A Strategic Coalignment." *Journal of Marketing* 51 (July 1987), pp. 1–14.

Harrigan, Kathryn Rudie. *Strategies for Declining Businesses.* Lexington, Mass.: Lexington Books, 1980.

Kerin, Roger A.; Vijay Mahajan; and P. Rajan Varadarajan. *Strategic Market Planning.* Boston: Allyn and Bacon, 1990.

Naisbitt, John. *Megatrends: Ten New Directions for Transforming Our Lives.* New York: Warner Books, 1984.

Porter, Michael E. *Competitive Strategy.* New York: Free Press, 1980.

Robock, Stefan H. "Political Risk: Identification and Assessment." *Columbia Journal of World Business,* July–August 1971, p. 7.

Standard & Poor's. *Analyst Handbook.* New York: Standard & Poor's Corporation, 1986.

Thomas, Philip S. "Environmental Analysis for Corporate Planning." *Business Horizons,* October 1974, p. 27.

CHAPTER 4

COMPETITOR ANALYSIS

OVERVIEW

To this point we have discussed defining competitors, the market, and customers. To complete the background needed for forecasting and strategy formulation, we now turn to detailed competitor analysis. As Porter (1979) said, "The essence of strategy formulation is coping with competition."

Competitor analysis has received more attention in the past few years for several reasons. First, many product categories are mature businesses, with slow or zero growth rates. In such markets, competitive pressures are intense as volume gains are derived from the other firms; that is, the market can be described as a zero-sum, or in a recession even a negative-sum, game. As a result, firms that understand their competitors' possible future strategies have an advantage over inward-oriented firms.

A second impetus for competitor analysis comes from the belief that product life cycles are shortening (Booz Allen & Hamilton Inc., 1982). Accordingly, there is more pressure on product managers to recoup investments in a shorter period, which makes errors of judgment about competition difficult to overcome.

Finally, the last decade has been perhaps the most turbulent period ever faced by marketing managers because of increased foreign competition, dramatic changes in technology and rates of innovation, large shifts in interest rates and inflation, changing customer tastes, and major political shifts (e.g., eastern Europe and Russia). When the environment contains so much uncertainty, it is important to keep abreast of changes in all factors exogenous to the firm, including competition.

Many companies have discovered the importance of competitor analysis:

- One Mitsubishi intelligence unit in the United States fills two floors of an office building in New York.

- Adolph Coors Co. keeps tabs on five major domestic competitors in detail and four foreign beer companies on a smaller scale.
- Motorola's information system contains data on the external environment, including competition; the data are used in strategic decision making, corporate planning and strategy, and business operations.
- Citicorp has an executive with the title manager of competitive intelligence.

Competitor intelligence gathering is not only for large companies. A recent example (*The Wall Street Journal,* April 1989) illustrates that small companies also can profit from such activity. The CEO of a small company turned a discussion with a customer into a problem for a competitor. The company, an importer of lamps and office furniture, had recently faced increased competition. The CEO learned from a retailer that one of the company's competitors had just raised the prices of some expensive lamps. The executive quickly relayed the information to the firm's field salespeople who used the information to win new business.

Why don't all firms have a formal reporting system designed to collect and analyze information about competitors? First, overconfidence about a product's continued success can reduce the willingness to collect competitor information. An impressive list of such manufacturers who were somewhat overconfident at one time (General Motors, Coca-Cola, McDonald's, IBM) can be produced along with the competitors who were ignored until they made significant inroads into their markets (Toyota, Pepsi, Burger King, Compaq). A second reason for insensitivity to competition is uncertainty about where to collect the necessary information and how to analyze it. This excuse grows weaker all the time with the proliferation of consultants specializing in competitive intelligence gathering, articles containing tips on where to collect information, and computerized databases containing articles about companies.

A final reason for not collecting competitive intelligence is an ethical consideration—the fear that either illegal methods or otherwise dirty tricks have to be used to obtain such information. Many examples of such behavior exist. Reverse engineering (copying) is a popular method for shortening lead times in introducing "me-too" products. Running phony help-wanted ads to lure and question competitors' employees is another frequently used ploy. However, the information obtained in such a manner can almost always be ethically obtained also.

At the minimum, firms should view methods for collecting information about competitors from a defensive perspective; that is, how they can prevent information about themselves from landing in the laps of important competitors. One company that takes this perspective seriously is Apple

Computer. Apple CEO John Sculley became so alarmed at the number of important secrets that were becoming public knowledge that he had a six-minute video made to be shown to new employees warning them about the implications of "loose lips" (*The Wall Street Journal*, October 1989).

Analyzing competitors requires a commitment to developing competitive strategy that includes a willingness to expend resources collecting such data. However, collecting the data is usually not the major problem facing marketing planners. As stated earlier, there are many sources of competitor intelligence. What is often lacking is a structure to guide the collection and analysis of the data and a clear idea of what questions the data should address.

This chapter proposes a structure for collecting, organizing, and analyzing competitor information that includes four areas of interest:

- What are the competitors' major objectives?
- What is the current strategy being employed to achieve the objectives?
- What are the capabilities of the competitors to implement their strategies?
- What are their likely future strategies?

The first three parts of the analysis are the background data needed to predict competitors' future strategies. The fourth aspect of competitor analysis could be called the bottom line. The purpose of examining the competitors is to forecast what they are likely to do over the next planning cycle. As mentioned previously, a marketing strategy for a product must account for these likely future strategies. Together, these four areas of information collection and analysis compose a fairly complete picture of the competitors' activities.

Many analysts prefer to treat your own company separately and perform an "internal capabilities" or other similar analysis and consider only outside competitors in the competitive analysis. We intentionally include the company itself in the competitor analysis for two reasons. First, considering your own company as "special" creates a tendency toward an inward rather than an outward orientation. Second, it is not absolute strengths and weaknesses but relative ones that determine success, so it is important to get a comparative picture on as many important aspects as possible.

In performing a competitive analysis, some data may be hard or even impossible to obtain, thus leading to either blanks in certain portions of the analysis or very qualitative information (e.g., product quality is "high"). This is inevitable and should both be expected and serve as a guide to possible directions for future information gathering.

ASSESSING THE COMPETITORS' CURRENT OBJECTIVES

The first step in competitor analysis is to attempt to assess the current objectives for the major competitor brands. An assessment of current objectives provides valuable information concerning the intended aggressiveness of the competitors. It also provides a context within which to assess the capabilities of the competitors; that is, does the firm marketing brand A have the resources to successfully pursue such an objective?

When discussing the idea of objectives, it is important to define the term precisely, for there are many different types of objectives. In the context of marketing planning, three basic brand objectives can be identified. The *growth objective* usually implies growing the brand in terms of either units or market share with profit conditions being secondary. The *hold objective* could also be termed a consolidation objective. A hold scenario might be logical for a brand that is losing market share, in that a reasonable first step in reversing its fortunes is to put a brake on the slide. Finally, the *harvest scenario* could also be termed a *milking* objective. Here, profit is of paramount importance.

At the brand level, objectives are typically stated in terms of either market share or profits. At the corporate level, return on investment or other more aggregate statistics become more relevant.

Determining Competitor Objectives

While a brand's objectives determine to a great extent what strategies will be pursued and, hence, what actions will be taken in the marketplace, it usually does not take a substantial amount of research to uncover them. What is required is sensitivity to competitors' actions through observation, salesperson call reports, and so on.

Let us consider the two major options outlined above—the growth versus harvest choice. If a competitor's brand is being pushed to improve its market position at the expense of short-term profits, then some of the following are likely to occur: product upgrades, a cut in price, increased advertising expenditures, increased promotional activity both to consumer and trade, or increased distribution expenses. In other words, a firm that is trying to expand a brand's market share will be actively spending money on market-related activities and/or reducing price. Such actions can be easily monitored by the brand managers, advertising account representatives, and other parties with access to information about the rival brand's actions.

Brands being harvested would be marketed in the opposite way. An increase in a competitor's price, decreases in marketing budgets, and so on, can be interpreted as a retreat (perhaps only temporary) from active competition in the market. While exact estimates of the size of the share loss expected cannot be obtained, it is not difficult to establish the direction of the objective.

Two other factors are relevant to the assessment of competitors' objectives. First, the objectives of a foreign brand or a product marketed by a firm with a foreign parent are often affected by the country of origin. In many cases, such firms have financial backing from a government or major banks and are not as concerned with short-term losses as they are with establishing a viable market position or obtaining foreign currency. Thus, depending on the competitor, cues concerning the competitor brand's objectives can be obtained from the geographical home of the parent firm.

A second relevant factor is whether the ownership of the competitor firm is private or public. Since the former do not have to account to stockholders, long-term profits may be more important than showing positive quarterly returns. On the other hand, if a family depends on the firm for current income, profits may be more important than market share. In these cases, knowledge of the ownership situation provides vital cues concerning likely objectives.

A less apparent level of objectives can be deduced from a firm's operating philosophy and procedures. For example, a firm that seeks to minimize capital investment will be slow to respond to a competitor that makes a heavy capital outlay (e.g., as Emery Air Freight was when Federal Express bought its own planes in the mid-1970s). Similarly, firms that compensate their sales staff based on a percent of sales commission indicate that volume (rather than profitability) is a key objective. In fact, the key performance measure (e.g., return on fixed assets) often has a distinct influence on a firm's behavior.

In sum, estimates of the objectives pursued by competitors provide important information for the development of strategy. A brand that is being aggressive in its pursuit of market share must be viewed as a different type of competitor than one that is primarily attempting to maximize profits. The latter brand would clearly be vulnerable to an attack against its customers, while a confrontation with the former brand might be avoided.

This type of analysis has been profitably applied. During the late 1970s, Coca-Cola was primarily concerned with holding market share and improving profits. Pepsi-Cola, on the other hand, viewed Coke's relative passivity as an opportunity and became more aggressive, gaining share points and improving its position versus Coke in store sales, which it still maintains. Miller's successful attack on Budweiser during the 1970s was prompted by a similar observation.

ASSESSING THE COMPETITORS' CURRENT STRATEGIES

The second stage in competitor analysis is to determine how the competitors are attempting to achieve their objectives. This question is addressed by examining their past and current strategies.

Marketing Strategy

Many authors have attempted to define the concept of strategy. At the brand level, a marketing strategy can be thought of in terms of three major components: target market selection, core strategy (i.e., differential advantage), and implementation (i.e., supporting marketing mix).

The first major component is the description of the market segment(s) to which the competing brands are being targeted. Consumer market segments can be described in various ways, as shown in Figure 4–1 (see also Chapter 5). Since few brands are mass marketed (i.e., marketed to all potential customers), the key point here is to determine which group(s) each brand has targeted. This is important from the perspectives of avoiding segments where there may be intense competition and determining undertargeted segments, which may represent opportunities.

Typically, target markets are fairly easy to determine. First, customers self-select themselves as targets based on the product/service itself. Second, companies often reveal the target. Sometimes they do this explicitly in annual reports, 10Ks, speeches, and other public pronouncements. Other times the target can be deduced from marketing mix decisions. Distribution choices disproportionately serve different types of customers as do different pricing strategies. Media advertising helps define the target both by demographics of the media and the copy appeal used. When combined with sales data (such as the brand-switching data described in Chapter 2), this can lead to a clear description of market targets by competitor and hence identification of particularly close competitors.

The second strategy component is what is called the core strategy (Luck and Prell, 1968). This is the basis on which the rival is competing, that is, its key claimed differential advantage(s). This critical component of strategy usually forms the basic selling proposition around which the brand's promotion is formed. It could also be called the brand's *positioning*.

Brand managers essentially have a choice between two types of differential advantages: price/cost based and product feature based. In other words, brands are usually positioned on price or quality dimensions. Concentration on price follows the classic approach developed by the Boston Consulting Group (Henderson, 1980), which advocates taking advantage of

FIGURE 4–1

Approaches to Segmenting Consumer Markets

Variables	Typical Breakdowns
Geographic:	
Region	Pacific; Mountain; West North Central; West South Central; East North Central; East South Central; South Atlantic; Middle Atlantic; New England
County size	A; B; C; D
City or SMSA size	Under 5,000; 5,000–19,999; 20,000–49,999; 50,000–99,999; 100,000–249,999; 250,000–499,999; 500,000–999,999; 1,000,000–3,999,999; 4,000,000 or over
Density	Urban; suburban; rural
Climate	Northern; southern
Demographic:	
Age	Under 6; 6–11; 12–17; 18–34; 35–49; 50–64; 65+
Sex	Male; female
Family size	1–2, 3–4, 5+
Family life cycle	Young, single; young, married, no children; young, married, youngest child under 6; young, married, youngest child 6 or over; older, married, with children; older, married, no children under 18; older, single; other
Income	Under $10,000; $10,000–$19,999; $20,000–$29,999; . . .
Occupation	Professional and technical; managers, officials and proprietors; clerical, sales; craftspeople, supervisors; operatives; farmers; retired; students; housewives; unemployed
Education	Grade school or less; some high school; graduated high school; some college; graduated college
Religion	Catholic; Protestant; Jewish; other
Race	White; black; Asian
Nationality	American; British; French; German; Eastern European; Scandinavian; Italian; Spanish; Latin American; Middle Eastern; Japanese; and so on
Social class	Lower-lower; upper-lower; lower-middle; middle-middle; upper-middle; lower-upper; upper-upper
Personality:	
Compulsiveness	Compulsive; noncompulsive
Gregariousness	Extrovert; introvert
Autonomy	Dependent; independent
Conservatism	Conservative; liberal; radical
Authoritarianism	Authoritarian; democratic
Leadership	Leader; follower
Ambitiousness	High achiever; low achiever
Values	SRI VALS Typology (Riche, 1989), Rokeach's 18 terminal and instrumental values (1973); List of Values (Kahle, 1986)
Buyer behavior:	
Usage rate	Nonuser; light user; medium user; heavy user
Readiness stage	Unaware; aware; interested; intending to try; trier; regular buyer
Benefits sought	Economy; status; dependability
End use	Varies with the product
Brand loyalty	None; weak; strong
Marketing-factor sensitivity	Quality; price; service; advertising; sales promotion

the experience curve that drives down unit costs and provides the ability to cut prices and maintain margins over time. While cost cutting does not necessarily imply declining prices, the brand wishing to claim a differential advantage based on price must be in a competitively superior position in terms of unit costs. The quality differential advantage, heavily advocated by Peters and Austin (1985), is a claim to be superior on some other product dimension, such as service, packaging, and delivery. For such a core strategy to be successful, customers must value the characteristics claimed as advantages and the differential must be maintained for a significant period of time without being copied.

Quality differential advantages can often be *perceived* rather than *actual* differences. For example, IBM's core strategy since its inception has been service based. This is an actual differential advantage because it can be supported by hard data (e.g., number of field service representatives, mean response time, and so on). On the other hand, Pepsi's claimed differential over Coke relates to its "younger generation" appeal; that is, drink Pepsi if you want to drink what younger people drink. Such positioning is outside the domain of physical product differences but is nonetheless effective in differentiating Pepsi from Coke. Physical product differences are often stressed in industrial, durable, or new, frequently purchased product strategies. Mature, frequently purchased products that are physically similar or commodities often emphasize perceptual differences.

The final strategy component of competitors that must be assessed is the supporting marketing mix. The mix provides insight into the basic strategy of the competitor as well as specific tactical decisions. The areas to consider follow.

Pricing

Pricing is a highly visible element of a competitor's marketing mix; therefore, several questions can be addressed. For example, if a brand's differential advantage is price based, is the list price uniform in all markets? If the strategy is quality based, what is the price differential claimed? Are discounts being offered? In general, any price-related information pertaining to the implementation of the aforementioned strategy is relevant.

Promotion

With respect to sales management, what kinds of selling approaches are used? Are the salespeople being aggressive in obtaining new accounts? In terms of advertising, what media are being used? What creative strategies? What timing pattern? Sales promotion questions are also important; for example, which types and how often?

Distribution

Have the channels of distribution shifted? Is the brand being emphasized in certain channels? Is the manufacturer of the competing brand changing the entire system; for example, by opening its own retail outlets or using more direct marketing?

Product/Service Capabilities

A major determinant of a company's capabilities, at least in the short run, is the physical makeup of its product/service offering, which is in general less easily changed than, say, price or advertising. Products filled with expensive parts are unlikely to be positioned as a low-end product. Similarly physical properties (e.g., stability under high temperatures, moldability, corrosion resistance, durability of packaging) go a long way toward dictating target uses and hence strategy. Many engineering plastics markets segment themselves on the basis of physical properties (e.g., Du Pont's Delrin versus Celanese's Celcon), with different applications dominated by different companies' offerings. Hence, at a minimum, the competitive product offerings (that is, the physical product/service plus how it is presented and sold) should be compared.

Perhaps equally important is the image associated with companies. This image (or brand equity) enables some companies to compete, for example, at the high end of the market even though their product is at best equivalent in quality. By the same token, unknown brands are often assumed to be of inferior quality even when they are not. Quality is usually eventually observable, so perceptions tend toward objective quality in most markets. The convergence, however, may be slow (as in the slow acceptance of Japanese cars in the United States and now the difficulty American manufacturers have in convincing customers of their improved quality). Still, the gap between objective and perceived quality provides a predictor of likely future movement and strategy. Thus, any competitive analysis should include information on perceived quality and satisfaction among current users.

How to Assess Competitors' Strategies

It should be emphasized at this point that detailed information about competitors is not yet necessary. Up to this stage in the competitor analysis process, all that is required are qualitative assessments of objectives and strategies.

Recall that the two key elements of a strategy are the segments appealed to and the core strategy. For industrial products, both can be easily determined by examining three sources of information: company sales literature, your own sales force, and trade advertising. The former provides information about the core strategy; brochures usually go into detail about differences between the firm's product and those of competitors. Even if the sales literature provides no direct comparison between brands, it should indicate the brand's major strengths. A firm's own sales force can provide data concerning targeted companies or industries. Much of this is of an informal nature resulting from contacts, trade show discussions, and the like. Finally, trade advertising is useful for discovering both the segments being targeted and the differential advantage touted. The latter can be determined directly from the copy, while the former can be at least partially determined by the publication in which the ad appears.

For consumer goods, simply tracking competitors' ads provides most of the necessary information. Television ads can be examined in terms of message (differential advantage) and program (target segment). TV advertising is useful for determining the core strategy. Similarly, print advertising can provide equivalent information but with more elaboration.

For example, consider the copy for a print ad for 1-2-3® from Lotus® shown in Figure 4–2 obtained from *Fortune* magazine. At least part of Lotus' strategy can be determined by utilizing both the fact that the ad appeared in *Fortune* and the copy itself. The target market for this ad can be determined from demographics of *Fortune's* readership and the copy, which illustrates a business application of the software. The claimed differential advantage is the additional productivity obtainable by using Lotus. This is only part of the overall strategy for the product because other ads could be oriented toward different segments with possibly different claimed advantages.

Information concerning implementation of current strategies is also easily found. Pricing-related information can be obtained from basic market observation; that is, distributors, salespeople, customers, advertising agencies, or even a firm's own employees acting as consumers can be the sources of pricing data. Promotion, distribution, and product-related facts can be obtained from similar sources. In other words, as in the case of objective determination, it takes only market sensitivity to assess much of the competitive activity rather than sophisticated management information systems.

One very apparent but often overlooked source of information is being a customer and/or stockholder of the competitors. Both customers and stockholders get special mailings and information that makes strategy assessment easier. Also, personal use of competitors' products often provides a feeling for them that does not come through even the best prepared research. Thus, policies that forbid or discourage the use of competitive products are usually foolish.

FIGURE 4–2
Determining Strategy from Print Ads

"Before 1-2-3 we used to guess."

A major California vineyard could never quite match the demand for their wines to their annual crop yield.

Two years ago they began using 1-2-3® to more accurately predict vineyard harvests by grape variety. Now they have the right grapes to produce more of their best-selling wines.

A real estate developer who used to guess at how a change in the amortization schedule, interest rates or the tax code would affect cash flow on her properties, now uses 1-2-3.

Now she knows for certain.

A large mail-order house specializing in outdoor clothing and equipment once relied on instinct to develop new products for their customers.

Now they rely on 1-2-3. Last year, they generated a 30% increase in sales.

A major cranberry cooperative has a better handle on crop yields, inventory and fruit harvests since using 1-2-3.

A leading insurance company has tighter control over relocation expenses for transferred executives using 1-2-3.

There's a surgeon in Boston who has developed a better way to monitor his patients' vital signs using 1-2-3.

A large southern utility has better control over the distribution and pricing of its natural gas.

An airline now keeps better track of passenger miles thanks to 1-2-3.

How much good could 1-2-3 do for your business?

At this point, you can only guess.

"1-2-3. The ultimate business tool."

This year an estimated one million people will discover how much more productive they can be using the premier spreadsheet, graphics and database software: 1-2-3 from Lotus.®

1-2-3 from Lotus is the best tested, best supported, most proven personal computer business software in the world. And we've just made it even better with new 1-2-3.

Shouldn't you be using it?

Printed ad. © 1985, Lotus Development Corporation. 1-2-3 and Lotus are registered trademarks of Lotus Development Corporation. Used with permission.

Technological Strategy

Another important task is to assess the technological strategies of the major competitors; that is, how they approach market conditions. This can be done using the framework of Maidique and Patch (1978), who suggest that six decisions need to be made.

1. Technology selection or specialization.
2. Level of competence.
3. Sources of capability: internal versus external.
4. R&D investment level.
5. Competitive timing: initiate versus respond.
6. R&D organization and policies.

These decisions generally lead to four basic strategies, each of which has different requirements for success (see Figure 4–3). For example, consider the blank audiocassette market in the early 1970s. This was the

FIGURE 4–3
Typical Functional Requirements of Alternative Technological Strategies

	R&D	Manufacturing	Marketing	Finance	Organization	Timing
First to market	Requires state-of-the-art R&D	Emphasis on pilot and medium-scale manufacturing	Emphasis on stimulating primary demand	Requires access to risk capital	Emphasis on flexibility over efficiency; encourage risk taking	Early-entry inaugurates the product life cycle
Second to market	Requires flexible, responsive, and advanced R&D capability	Requires agility in setting up manufacturing medium scale	Must differentiate the product; stimulate secondary demand	Requires rapid commitment of medium to large quantities of capital	Combine elements of flexibility and efficiency	Entry early in growth stage
Late to market or cost minimization	Requires skill in process development and cost-effective product	Requires efficiency and automation for large-scale production	Must minimize selling and distribution costs	Requires access to capital in large amounts	Emphasis on efficiency and hierarchical control; procedures rigidly enforced	Entry during late growth or early maturity
Market segmentation	Requires ability in applications, custom engineering, and advanced product design	Requires flexibility on short to medium runs	Must identify and reach favorable segments	Requires access to capital in medium or large amounts	Flexibility and control required in serving different customers' requirements	Entry during growth stage

early stage of the product life cycle with no major competitors. Gillette's Safety Razor Division was considering entering this market as was Memorex, a manufacturer of computer tape and related products. While Gillette had slight competitive advantages over Memorex in marketing and finance, it was at a disadvantage in terms of R&D and manufacturing. The end result was a success for Memorex and a Gillette failure in test market (see the Harvard Business School case, "Gillette Safety Razor Division: The Blank Cassette Project" for more details).

At this point in the analysis, it is often useful to summarize the products of the major competitors. Figure 4–4 provides a general format that is useful both for summarizing the results and for communicating them.

Management Processes

One important aspect of competitor analysis focuses on the processes and procedures used. Currently, a major trend is the development of quality pro-

FIGURE 4–4

Format for Competitive Product Offering Analysis

	Own Brands 1 . . . K_0	Competitor A Brand 1 . . . K_A	Competitor B Brand 1 . . . K_B
Product:			
Actual quality			
Features			
Quality image			
Target segment:			
Who			
Where			
When			
Why			
Place:			
Distribution method			
Distribution coverage			
Promotion:			
Total effort ($)			
Methods			
Advertising:			
Strategy/copy			
Media			
Timing			
Total effort			
Price:			
Retail			
To trade			

grams such as Total Quality Management (TQM). Users of TQM focus on a variety of activities including benchmarking their programs against those of world-class companies (not necessarily limited to those in their industry), assessing customer satisfaction, empowering employees to act with more initiative, speeding up product design (reducing cycle time), simplifying production processes, and selecting and working with a small number of suppliers. Other programs such as the House of Quality guide product development by linking desired customer benefits to engineering and parts specifications early in the design process. Use of these, or any other procedures, indicates likely decisions as well as a sense of what a company is unlikely to do.

ASSESSING COMPETITORS' CAPABILITIES

It is assumed that evidence has been accumulated thus far concerning competitors' current objectives and strategies. Recall that the ultimate goal of this analysis is to predict the competitors' likely future strategies. While past actions are often a good predictor, so are current capabilities.

What to Collect

Several frameworks have been proposed to indicate which information to collect about competitors (Ansoff, 1979; Hussey, 1971). One that has been used extensively was developed by Rothschild (1979). He divides the necessary information into five mutually exclusive categories concerned with the competitors' "abilities" to conceive and design, to produce, to market, to finance, and to manage.

Ability to Conceive and Design

This category attempts to measure the quality of the firms' new product development efforts. Clearly, a firm with a high ability to develop new products is a more serious long-term threat than a firm that has not been innovative. The use of such procedures as TQM and the House of Quality generally improves product design capabilities.

Ability to Produce

In this category, we attempt to determine the production capabilities of the firms. For a service business, this category might be termed *ability to deliver the service*. For example, a firm that is operating at capacity for a product is not as much a threat to expand in the short run as is a firm that has slack capacity, assuming a substantial period is required to bring new capacity on-line.

Ability to Market

How aggressive, inventive, and so on are the firms in marketing their products? Do they have a strong presence in key distribution channels? A competitor could have strong product development capabilities and slack capacity but be ineffective at marketing.

Ability to Finance

The lack of availabile financial resources clearly acts as a constraint to being an effective competitor. While financial ratios are key pieces of information, how the competitor firm shifts its resources between products is also critical.

Ability to Manage

Several years ago, Procter & Gamble replaced the manager of its U.S. coffee business with the coffee general manager from the United Kingdom. This new manager had a reputation for developing new products: in 15 months, for example, he oversaw the launch of four new brands, which was above average for the company. The message to competitors such as General Foods was clear. In general, the characteristics of key managers provide signals to competitors concerning likely strategies.

WHERE TO FIND THE INFORMATION

Examples of specific bits of information that should be collected are shown in Figure 4–5. While the list is not exhaustive, it highlights major areas that should be researched.

The search for information necessary to cover the areas indicated in Figure 4–5 is extensive. Typically, the search involves the collection of both primary (i.e., data not already collected by some other institution) and secondary data. A brief listing of some of the secondary sources is given in Figure 4–6 (see p. 77).

A prime source of secondary information is a computer database. In today's world of advancing computer technology, much information about competitors can be found using dial-up computer databases and information on compact disks. Since these are changing rapidly, a visit to a local

FIGURE 4–5
Competitor Capabilities

A. Ability to conceive and design
   1. Technical resources
      a. Concepts
      b. Patents and copyrights
      c. Technological sophistication
      d. Technical integration
   2. Human resources
      a. Key people and skills
      b. Use of external technical groups
   3. R&D funding
      a. Total
      b. Percentage of sales
      c. Consistency overtime
      d. Internally generated
      e. Government supplied
   4. Technological strategy
      a. Specialization
      b. Competence
      c. Source of capability
      d. Timing: initiate vs. imitate
   5. Management processes
      a. TQM
      b. House of Quality
B. Ability to produce
   1. Physical resources
      a. Capacity
      b. Plant
         (1) Size
         (2) Location
         (3) Age
      c. Equipment
         (1) Automation
         (2) Maintenance
         (3) Flexibility
      d. Processes
         (1) Uniqueness
         (2) Flexibility
      e. Degree of integration
   2. Human resources
      a. Key people and skills
      b. Work force
         (1) Skills mix
         (2) Unions
C. Ability to market
   1. Sales force
      a. Skills
      b. Size
      c. Type
      d. Location
   2. Distribution network
      a. Skills
      b. Type
   3. Service and sales policies

FIGURE 4–5 (*concluded*)

    4. Advertising
       a. Skills
       b. Type
    5. Human resources
       a. Key people and skills
       b. Turnover
    6. Funding
       a. Total
       b. Consistency over time
       c. Percentage of sales
       d. Reward systems
D. Ability to finance
    1. Long term
       a. Debt/equity ratio
       b. Cost of debt
    2. Short term
       a. Cash or equivalent
       b. Line of credit
       c. Type of debt
       d. Cost of debt
    3. Liquidity
    4. Returns from operations
       a. Margin
       b. Profits
       c. Cash flow
       d. Return on sales, assets, marketing expenditures
       e. Inventory, receivables turnover
    5. Human resources
       a. Key people and skills
       b. Turnover
    6. System
       a. Budgeting
       b. Forecasting
       c. Controlling
E. Ability to manage
    1. Key people
       a. Objectives and priorities
       b. Values
       c. Reward systems
    2. Decision making
       a. Location
       b. Type
       c. Speed
    3. Planning
       a. Type
       b. Emphasis
       c. Time span
    4. Staffing
       a. Longevity and turnover
       b. Experience
       c. Replacement policies
    5. Organization
       a. Centralization
       b. Functions
       c. Use of staff

FIGURE 4–6
Representative Sources of Information about Competitors

	Public	Trade/Professionals	Government	Investors
What competitors say about themselves	Advertising Promotional materials Press releases Speeches Books Articles Personnel changes Want ads Customer communications	Manuals Technical papers Licenses Patents Courses Seminars	Security and Exchange Commission reports FTC filings Applications and permit filings Patent filings	Annual meetings Annual reports Prospectuses Stock and bond issues
What others say about them	Books Articles Case studies Consultants Newspaper reporters Environmental groups Consumer groups Unions Recruiting firms	Suppliers/ vendors Trade press Industry study Customers Subcontractors Consultants	Lawsuits Antitrust State and federal agencies National plans Government programs	Security analyst reports Industry studies Credit reports

university or public library will provide information about the latest resources. Some books also focus on the collection of competitor information. Examples are books by Fuld (1988), Gilad and Gilad (1989), and Prescott (1989). Companies specializing in this type of data collection, such as FIND/SVP in New York, can also be helpful.

An interesting dimension of Figure 4–6 is the breakdown of who does the "talking." Much of what can be determined about competitors' resources can be obtained from the firms themselves. For example, a firm will give away information about a future new plant location in a want ad seeking job applicants. A company that boasts about new products in an article in the business press gives rivals lead time to copy it. Plant tours are often good sources of information for competitors. However, some companies, such as Kellogg, are eliminating such tours as defensive measures.

Competitors themselves are often good sources of information because they do not take adequate defensive postures to prevent other competitors from obtaining sometimes critical information. A firm that does not actively scan its competitors' activities may not be sensitized to defending itself. Alternatively, a firm taking active positions in terms of information dissemination about itself could be doing it consciously for several reasons. First, it could be trying to give signals to competitors both as a warning ("this is my turf ") or to deceive. Second, the information is often "marketed" to security analysts and other elements of the financial community who either trade the company's stock, determine its creditworthiness, or provide capital. Finally, the information has value for the morale of employees, who tend to prefer working for a firm that is visible and dynamic.

Foreign competitors are often a difficult target for information collection. Some sources of information are unique to foreign competitors. One strategy is to subscribe to foreign-language newspapers from towns near competitor manufacturing facilities, headquarters, or service locations. Often, the local media have useful bits of information such as help-wanted notices, personnel shifts, and so forth that do not make international publications. Alternatively, special services that provide such local information include Overseas Courier Service, which tracks Japanese companies, and the German News Company for Europe. Foreign brokerage firms based in the United States can also be useful sources of information. International chambers of commerce or foreign trade organizations in the United States also provide information about companies based in their home countries.

WHAT TO DO WITH THE INFORMATION

This is the stage at which many competitor analysis efforts fall flat. What do we do with all the information collected? A useful format for synthesizing the large quantity of information is needed.

A first step toward making some sense out of all the data is to construct a table patterned after that shown in Figure 4–7. This forces the manager to boil down the information to its essential parts and provides a quick summary of a large amount of data. One column of the table is labeled "Own Company." This forces an internal assessment; the firm performing the analysis ultimately must see how its resources compare with those of its competitors.

Figure 4–8 presents a matrix illustrating this data simplification for the hard-disk-drive industry. As can be seen, all the information previously prescribed cannot be gathered in a limited period. In addition, often qualitative assessments and estimates based on partial information must be made. A quick glance at the matrix shows how useful this format can be; it is easy to see that Seagate has developed its market leadership primarily through extensive research and development expenditures, Quantum has

FIGURE 4–7
Competitive Capability Assessment

	Competing Firm				Own Company
	A	B	C	D	
Conceive and design:					
• Technical resources					
• Human resources					
• Funding					
•					
•					
•					
•					
Produce:					
• Physical resources					
• Human resources					
•					
•					
•					
•					
Finance:					
• Debt					
• Liquidity					
• Cash flow					
• Budget system					
•					
•					
•					
Market:					
• Sales force					
• Distribution					
• Service and sales policies					
• Advertising					
• Human resources					
• Funding					
•					
Manage:					
• Key people					
• Decision process					
• Planning					
• Staffing					
• Organization structure					
•					
•					

FIGURE 4–8
Competitor Capabilities Matrix for Hard Disk Drives (c. 1988)

Competitors' Capabilities	Conner	Miniscribe	Quantum	Seagate
Ability to develop:				
R&D budget (in $ MM)	3.5	18.1	12.1	50.1
R&D to sales (percent)	3 (low)	5 (medium)	10 (high)	4 (medium)
Historical record	Excellent	Average	Excellent	Average
Employees	72	363		
Patents	Spindle Motor	Rack-Pinion Actuator		
Ability to manufacture:				
Capacity	179,000 sq ft	640,000 sq ft	160,000 sq ft	
Automation	Poor	Good	Excellent	Average
Employees (direct labor)	724	3822	172	
Skills	Average	Good	Good	Average
Ability to market:				
Sales force	22	61	87	
Inventories (days)	96 (Poor)	114 (Poor)	36 (excellent)	66 (average)
Customer diversification	Poor	Excellent	Poor	Mixed
OEM relationship	Strong	Good	Poor	Strong
Ability to finance:				
Cash position	Average	Poor	Excellent	Excellent
Debt to equity	Low	High	Low	Low
Profitability	High	Excellent	Questionable	Average
Ability to manage:				
Historically	Untested	Good	Erratic	Good
Experience of CEO	Excellent	Good	Average	Excellent

the most automated manufacturing capabilities, Miniscribe has the largest capacity, and one of Conner Peripheral's main strengths is its new product development record.

Figure 4–9 presents an example of a competitor analysis in the wine industry. Figure 4–10 illustrates the use of further simplification of the analysis. This entails (1) determining key factors for success in the business in question and, (2) based on the data from Figure 4–9, rating the competitors along those key factors or dimensions. This simplification produces clearly identifiable conclusions. Gallo has a significant competitive advantage on almost every key dimension, while Canandaigua is clearly in an inferior position in the market. Thus, a two-step data-reduction approach often results in a clarified picture of the competitive situation and relatively clear directions for strategy development.

ASSESSING A COMPETITOR'S WILL

Even the strongest competitor can be overcome if it is not committed to the market. Similarly, even a weak competitor can cause massive damage if it is fanatically committed.

At some point, it is crucial to assess the competitors' strength of will or commitment. This requires going beyond objectives (What do they want?) to assess the intensity with which they approach the task (How badly do they want it?). Most competitions involve several key times at which each competitor has the choice of backing down or continuing the fight. In assessing the likelihood of a competitor continuing the fight (an act that sometimes is not "rational" in a profit sense), one should assess:

1. How crucial is this product to the firm? The more crucial in terms of sales and profits, number of employees, or strategic thrust, the more committed most companies will be to it. This helps explain why efforts to unseat a market leader by attacking the heart of its market provoke violent reactions ("If those . . . think they can take our market without a fight, . . .") whereas a strategy that nibbles away at secondary markets is more likely to go unmatched ("Well, it only represents 2 percent of our sales, so we shouldn't be too concerned about it").
2. How visible is the commitment to the market? It may be difficult to admit you are wrong. A good example of this is Exxon's Office Systems Division, which was clearly in trouble for a long time before it was sold in 1985.
3. Are the best employees and managers involved, or is the second or third team in charge? How aggressive are the managers? Some

FIGURE 4–9

Competitor Capabilities Matrix for Wine (c. 1989)

	Gallo	Heublein	Vintners	Canandaigua	Seagram
Commitment to wine market	Deeply committed	Questionable	Deeply committed	Committed	Somewhat committed
Major brands	Gallo, Bartles & James, Carlo Rossi, Andre, Thunderbird	Inglenook, Almaden, Lancer	Paul Masson, Taylor (California and New York), Great Western, Partager	Richards Wild Irish Rose, Sun Country Cooler	Seagrams Wine Cooler, Perrier-Jouet Champagne, Mondavi & Sons
Ability to develop new products	Excellent in low end	Very good	Poor	Good	Excellent
Brand recognition	Excellent in low end	Very good	Very good	Good	Very good
Ability to market: Advertising	Industry leader willingness to invest heavily	Parent is talented marketer	Unproven	Questionable	Talented
Philosophy	Out-muscle the competition	Undetermined	Return to basics	Undetermined	Become premium beverage leader
Adaptability to changing markets	Good but becoming more risk averse	Undetermined	Poor	Poor	Very good
Ability to finance: Cash position	Unknown but believed excellent	Excellent	Poor	Poor	Excellent
Debt levels/debt potential	Undetermined	Undetermined	Highly leveraged; perhaps at limit	Can borrow on assets	Acceptable debt levels/large debt potential
Ability to produce	Large production ability, low acreage	Undetermined	Good production ability	Good production ability	Undetermined
Leadership	Talented	Undetermined	Talented	Undetermined	Talented

FIGURE 4–10
Competitive Analysis Simplification: Wine

Criteria	Gallo	Heublein	Vintners	Canandaigua	Seagram
Commitment to wine	1	5	2	3	4
Financial strength	2	1	4	5	3
Brand awareness	1	2	3	5	4
Management ability	1	4	2	3	5

Highest = 1.
Lowest = 5.

people are more combative than others. The most combative opponents react with a fervor that makes reaching a business détente almost impossible.

Only by knowing how badly a competitor "wants it" can we successfully approach the next task, predicting future strategies.

PREDICTING FUTURE STRATEGIES

The manager is now armed with three sets of information about major competitors. First, we have assessed what their likely objectives are; that is, for what reward they are currently playing the game. Second, we have a view on their current strategy. Finally, we have some idea about their resources and abilities to compete. The final step is to put it all together and answer the question we started with: What are they likely to do in the future? In particular, we are interested in their likely strategies over the subsequent planning horizon, often a year.

One way to predict competitors' strategies does not employ the previously discussed information. Sometimes, competitors will actually disclose their likely future strategies through sources previously listed in Figure 4–6. For example, Warner-Lambert (Giges and Jervey, 1982) indicated that for its over-the-counter health-care products, including Myadec vitamins and Benylin cough syrup, it was going to redirect promotion from health-care professionals alone to consumers as well. This indicated a clear shift in strategy—a change in market segments to which it was appealing.

Often, however, the competition does not come right out and indicate what strategies it will pursue. In that case, subjective estimates are based on the information previously collected and analyzed. One way to approach the problem is to emulate what forecasters do with historical data. With historical observations on both a dependent variable to predict (in our context, a competitor's strategy) and independent variables useful for predicting the dependent variable (in our context, the resource variables), the forecaster might do one of two things. First, she or he might simply assume the trend will continue; that is, suppose that the only relevant information is the historical pattern of past strategies. For example, if a firm had a track record of selling brands with a premium image and high price, one could extrapolate into the future and assume this will continue. Similarly, if a brand has been appealing to increasingly mature consumers, a manager might presume the trend will continue. This trend approach assumes there is no information in the independent variables.

An alternative approach is for the forecaster to try to establish a cause-and-effect relationship between the resource variables and the strategy. In other words, the forecaster could try to link changes in resources or abilities to the strategies to be pursued.

Several examples help clarify this approach. Several years ago, Merrill Lynch spent heavily to bring in managers with package-goods experience to develop the markets for its financial services. Competitors (E. F. Hutton, Dean Witter) could forecast that this would result in an emphasis on market segmentation (pursuing high-potential customers) and increased spending on marketing-related activities such as advertising. Bethlehem Steel invested billions of dollars to upgrade its flat-rolled steel facilities. Competitors could forecast that this investment in highly efficient capacity would improve Bethlehem's ability to simultaneously cut price and protect margins. RCA tried for years to sell its Hertz subsidiary (it finally sold it in the mid-1980s to UAL, now Allegis Corporation). This resulted in RCA diverting marketing funds from Hertz to "fatten up" its bottom line and make it look more attractive to a potential buyer. Competitors of Hertz were, of course, delighted since it decreased Hertz's ability to market and therefore limited its strategic options. Finally, both Bell Labs and Du Pont spent considerable resources training employees in the marketing concept, suggesting a change in direction.

A third approach to strategy forecasting does not explicitly employ historical data but uses it in a different way. Corning Glass's highly profitable Corning Ware line was coming off patent. At the same time, several companies (Libby-Owens-Ford, Anchor Hocking) were looking at that business. Corning was interested in how a competitor would enter so it could preempt the entry strategy. To forecast the probable entry strategy, it asked senior managers to role-play (i.e., simulate) a competitor and determine how they would attack Corning Ware. This exercise provided useful defensive information to Corning.

Thus, a third approach to forecasting competitors' possible actions is to simulate them. One can take the existing data already collected, play the role of the competitor, and develop competitor action scenarios. Smith Kline did that when Tagamet, the largest-selling prescription drug in the world and the source of one third of Smith Kline's profits, was coming off patent. In this case, it knew who the competitor was going to be (Glaxo Holdings); Smith Kline prepared its salespeople for how it expected Glaxo to promote its drug, Zantac, in terms of differential advantage (fewer doses needed per day) and how to counteract arguments against Tagamet. This simulation approach has been highly effective.

When there are few competitors, it is possible to use a combination of game theory and decision trees to predict competitive behavior. To use these, we assume the objective of both firms is known and the same, such as annual profits. Then, for a particular decision, such as whether to cut versus maintain current prices, we can calculate the profitability to both parties as shown in Figure 4–11, which represents a "game" between the two competitors. Here we see that total profits are maximized if both maintain prices. Notice, however, that both parties are better off cutting prices if their competitor maintains them. This makes the situation inherently unstable and also makes prediction of competitor strategy crucial to maximizing profits.

In response to this situation, it is apparently in the best interest of both parties to collude to maintain prices and, if they are sophisticated, to divide the extra profits they gain proportionally to their respective gains. Assuming such a cartel is illegal or unstable, the key to understanding behavior is often to assume that one competitor moves first and the other responds. For example, the decision tree in Figure 4–12 depicts the situation where we move first and the competitor responds. Given the estimated response probabilities (which should be based on the competitor analysis), we can compute the expected results of the two decisions:

We cut price: $.9 (20) + .1 (180) = 36$.

We maintain price: $.3 (10) + .7 (100) = 73$.

FIGURE 4–11
Game Theory Illustration

Payoff matrix

	We cut prices	We maintain prices
They cut prices	30 = Their profits, 20 = Our profits	240, 10
They maintain prices	50, 180	160, 100

FIGURE 4–12

Conditional Strategy Probabilities

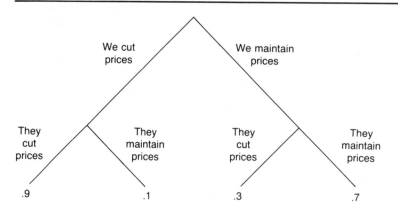

FIGURE 4–13

Expected Competitor Behavior

	Product Form Competitors		Product Category Competitors	
	Diet Coke	"Price"—Diet Colas (Vintage, C&C, . . .)	Coke	7UP
Objective				
Strategy				
Mix elements:				
Product				
Price				
Advertising				
Promotion				
Distribution				

Therefore, allowing for competitive response leads to the conclusion that, on average, we would be better off maintaining price.

While building decision trees is a correct way to proceed, it is unwieldy given multiple competitors and the many possible strategies that could be employed. Moreover, the probabilities needed are at best estimates. Consequently, as a first cut, it is often useful to simply predict the basic strategy of competitors. This can be done as suggested in Figure 4–13. Then, assuming we are contemplating an unexpected strategy, we can simply indicate the likely reactions of the competitors to various strategic alternatives as in Figure 4–14. While Figures 4–13 and 4–14 are much less elegant than

FIGURE 4–14
Expected Competitive Response

	Product Form Competitors		Product Category Competitors	
	Diet Coke	"Price"— Diet Colas	Coke	7UP
Environmental change: Overall demand Regulatory				
Competitive strategy change: 1. (e.g., new product) 2. (e.g., price cut)				

either game theory or decision tree analysis, they are both easier to use and a more appropriate reflection of the typical level of information available for competitor analysis.

SUMMARY

The analysis of competitors is a crucial element in preparing a sensible marketing plan. Only by knowing what the competitors are likely to do can a firm hope to choose an optimal strategy. Essentially, competitor analysis involves: (1) assessing their objectives, (2) determining their current strategies, (3) evaluating their capabilities, and (4) forecasting their future strategies. This is the marketing equivalent of scouting in sports. Given the effort put into scouting in such diverse sports as high school football and America's Cup racing, where the financial gain is limited, it seems only reasonable that a company dealing with a multimillion-dollar product would want to be at least as well prepared.

REFERENCES

Ansoff, H. Igor. *Corporate Strategy*. Hammondsworth, England: Penguin Books, 1979.

"At Apple Computer Proper Office Attire Includes a Muzzle." *The Wall Street Journal*, October 6, 1989.

Booz Allen & Hamilton Inc. *New Products Management for the 1980s*. Chicago: 1982.

"'Competitor Intelligence': A New Grapevine." *The Wall Street Journal*, April 12, 1989.

Fuld, Leonard M. *Monitoring the Competition.* New York: John Wiley & Sons, 1988.

Giges, Nancy, and Gay Jervey. "W-L Plans Major Outlays." *Advertising Age,* May 3, 1982, p. 3.

Gilad, Benjamin, and Tamar Gilad. "The Intelligence Audit." *Advances in Competitive Intelligence.* Ed. John Prescott. Vienna, Va.: Society of Competitive Intelligence Professionals, 1989, pp. 167–73.

Hauser, John, and Donald Clausing. "The House of Quality." *Harvard Business Review,* 66 (May–June 1988), pp. 63–73.

Henderson, Bruce D. "The Experience Curve Revisited." *Perspectives,* no. 220 (1980).

Hussey, D. E. *Introducing Corporate Planning.* Oxford, England: Pergamon Press, 1971.

Kahle, Lynn. "Alternative Measurement Approaches to Consumer Values: The List of Values (LOV) and Values and Life Styles (VALS)." *Journal of Consumer Research* 13 (December 1986), pp. 405–9.

Luck, David J., and Arthur E. Prell. *Market Strategy.* New York: Appleton-Century-Crofts, 1968.

Maidique, Modesto A., and Peter Patch. "Corporate Strategy and Technological Policy." Working Paper, Harvard Business School, 1978.

Mitchell, Arndt. *The Nine American Life Styles.* New York: Warner Books, 1983.

Peters, Thomas J., and Nancy Austin. *A Passion for Excellence: The Leadership Difference.* New York: Random House, 1985.

Porter, Michael E. "The Structure within Industries and Companies' Performance." *Review of Economics and Statistics* 61 (May 1979), pp. 214–27.

Prescott, John E., ed. *Advances in Competitive Intelligence.* Vienna, Va.: Society of Competitive Intelligence Professionals, 1989.

Riche, Martha Farnsworth. "Psychographics for the 1990s." *American Demographics,* 1989, pp. 25–31.

Rokeach, Milton. *The Nature of Human Value.* New York: Free Press, 1973.

Rothschild, William E. *Putting It All Together.* New York: AMACOM, 1979.

CHAPTER 5

CUSTOMER ANALYSIS

OVERVIEW

Customers are central to the practice of marketing because without customers, a business cannot survive. While this may appear to be clear or even trivial, many marketing managers have regretted not obtaining sufficient information about their customers in order to develop products or strategies that are consonant with their needs.

Marketing strategy development has at its core understanding customers. Strategy basically involves selecting among customers (and both implicitly and explicitly with which competitors to do battle). The strategy selection process can be described as five steps:

1. List/describe customers.
2. Form segments of customers.
3. Describe each segment.
4. Select which segments to concentrate on serving.
5. Develop programs to serve the selected segments.

Customer analysis is basically the completion of the first three steps.

This chapter describes some ways to structure a customer analysis. In this chapter, the term *customer* refers not just to current customers of a given firm but also to customers of competitors and current noncustomers of the product class. For useful planning to occur, one must consider the potential market for the product and not just its current market and customers.

Rarely will a single typical customer exist. Rather, each customer is to some degree unique. Since it is usually both time consuming and unprofitable to develop a strategy for each customer, some grouping of customers is required. This segmentation is the compromise between treating each customer as unique and assuming all customers are equal. Its purpose is to both provide insights and make marketing programs more efficient.

In this chapter, we suggest an approach to systematically considering who the customers are, how they can be described, and how they can be grouped (segmented) to facilitate strategic and tactical decision making. We begin by discussing what we need (or at least would like) to know about customers. Next, we examine in greater detail the general area of how and why customers decide what to purchase; this area often provides an accurate insight into the market. Then, methods for grouping customers into segments are described. Finally, we provide a general summary of and format for customer analysis.

WHAT WE NEED TO KNOW ABOUT CUSTOMERS

The best basis for customer analysis is the one that leads to the best decisions and therefore greatest profit. Since this is a fairly vacuous tautology, a manager must decide on the basis he or she thinks will be useful. The following text is a description of the most widely used bases (see Figure 5-1 for the overview). We pay particular attention to why they buy because of its importance and its central role in maintaining an outward, customer orientation.

Who Buys and Uses the Product

When a manager decides to analyze the customers in a market, the first question is, "Who are the customers?" For most industrial goods and many consumer goods, the "who" must be broken into (a) who buys it and (b) who uses it (the ultimate consumer), the identities of whom may be widely different. Consider purchases made by a purchasing agent. The end user may be an engineer who is mainly concerned with technical features, whereas the purchasing agent emphasizes cost and reliability of delivery. One reason for the success of Federal Express was that firm's ability to bypass the shipping clerk in the decision on how to send overnight packages by making the user the purchaser. Similarly, the purchase of cereal, toys, or fast-food meals is often made by an adult, whereas the user of the product is a child. McDonald's ads recognize this and attempt to target both the teenage market (with money of their own) and the "family meal" segment, where the child is likely to influence where the family goes to eat. This distinction also holds for goods sold for resale either directly or as a part of another product. In short, it is important to analyze both the immediate and ultimate customer.

FIGURE 5–1
What We Need to Know about Current and Potential Customers

1. Who they are:
   Purchaser
   User
2. What they buy:
   What they buy: Amount
   What they buy: Brand, features
   What they do with it: Usage situation
3. Where they buy.
4. When they buy:
   Time of year, month, week, day
   On sale/promotion versus full price
5. How they choose:
   Decision participants' roles
   Process
   Information sources; shopping locations
6. Why they select a product: Customer value:
   Functional attributes
   Service
   Image
   Brand equity
7. Will they buy it (again)?
   Satisfaction
   Intentions
8. Sensitivity to marketing mix:
   Product
   Price
   Distribution
   Advertising
   Promotion
   Service

Consumer Goods

The most obvious (and popular) basis for describing the customer is general characteristics. In the area of consumer goods, this usually means four general types of variables: demographic, socioeconomic, personality, and psychographics and values.

Demographic. The most commonly used demographics are age, sex, geographic location, and stage in the life cycle. These characteristics are relatively easy to ascertain. Unfortunately, they are (with obvious exceptions such as baby food) generally only weakly related to behavior, so demographic-based segments are often not very different in terms of behavior.

A number of services provide data on usage by demographic segmentation. For example, Simmons Market Research Bureau provides a breakdown of usage of consumer products based on age, income, and so on (as well as magazine readership, etc.). These cross-tabulated-style reports indicate where users can be found by using an index where 100 equals average usage. One category reported is snack cakes. Not surprisingly, usage is heaviest among less educated families with children (see Figure 5–2).

Socioeconomic. Socioeconomic variables include income and such related variables as education, occupation, and social class, with income and education generally being most useful. Again, as in the case of demographics, the relation between these variables and purchase behavior is fairly weak. For frequently purchased goods, demographic and socioeconomic variables typically account for less than 10 percent of the variation in purchase rates of a product category across households (Frank, Massy, and Wind, 1972; Massy, Frank, and Lodahl, 1968).

Personality. Given the relatively limited predictive power of demographic and socioeconomic variables, the fact that many people in marketing are trained in psychology, and the natural desire to find a general basis for dividing consumers that will be useful over many situations, it is not surprising that an attempt has been made to use personality traits as a basis for segmentation. Also not surprising, such traits as dominance and

FIGURE 5–2
Snack Cake Usage Rates*

	All Users	Heavy Users
Education of Female Head of Household		
Graduated from college	83	67
Attended college	94	93
Graduated from high school	105	105
Did not graduate from high school	107	118
Children in Household		
None	82	68
Under 2 years	117	140
2–5 years	126	161
6–11 years	131	157
12–17 years	130	160

* 100 = Average use

Source: Simmons Market Research Bureau.

aggressiveness are typically not highly related to ketchup consumption (see Kassarjian, 1971, for an extensive review of this area).

Psychographics and Values. Psychographics basically represent an evolution from general personality variables to attitudes and behaviors more closely related to consumption of goods and services. Psychographics, also known as lifestyle variables, generally fall into three categories: Activities (cooking, sports, and so on), Interests (art, music), and Opinions. (Consequently, we get the description AIO.) These have been widely used as bases for segmentation by many companies (e.g., General Foods) and also have been used as the basis for the creation of advertising themes by ad agencies (e.g., Needham, Harper, and Steers). Recently, many researchers have begun using the VALS typology (Values and Life Styles; Mitchell, 1983; see Figure 5–3) developed by SRI International as a basis for defining segments (e.g., New York Telephone used this to segment the market for decorator phones; Schiffman and Jones, 1983).

Another typology, the List of Values (LOV) Scale (Kahle, Beatty, and Homer, 1986), delineates nine basic values:

1. Self-respect.
2. Security.
3. Warm relationship with others.
4. Sense of accomplishment.
5. Self-fulfillment.
6. Sense of belonging.
7. Being well respected.
8. Fun and enjoyment.
9. Excitement.

FIGURE 5–3
The VALS Segments

VAL	VALS 2
Inner-directed consumers	Principle-oriented
Societally Conscious	Fulfilleds
Experientials	Believers
I-Am-Me Consumers	Status-oriented
Outer-directed consumers	Achievers
Achievers	Strivers
Emulators	Action-oriented
Belongers	Experiencers
Need-driven consumers	Makers
Sustainers	Strugglers
Survivors	

This typology provides some understanding of different purchase patterns, such as among consumer durables (Corfman, Lehmann, and Narayanan, 1991).

While general segmentation schemes may be useful for some products, a more tailored approach is generally superior. Still, general segmentation schemes and customer analysis remain potentially useful. As an example of this, and in recognition of the growing international nature of markets, in 1989 Backer Spielvogel Bates Worldwide introduced GLOBAL-SCAN, a survey of 15,000 adults in 14 countries. This survey included cultural attitudes, media behavior, and brand purchase behavior in addition to basic demographics. This analysis produced five basic categories of people: Strivers, Achievers, Pressured, Adapters, and Traditionals. Other schemes developed in Europe include CCA from France (Socio-Styles-Systeme) and the Swiss-based International *Research Institute* for *Social Change*'s RISC system.

Industrial Goods

For industrial goods, the focus has been on firm characteristics such as size of company, location, and sales, which are the logical equivalent of demographic and socioeconomic variables used for consumer products.

Probably the most widely used basis for industrial segmentation in the United States is the Standard Industrial Classification (SIC) coding system. This system, which is popular largely because of its availability, is maintained by the U.S. government as a basis for tracking output by industry. Two-digit codes indicate major industry groups (e.g., 34 is fabricated metal products), three digits indicate broadly defined industries (e.g., 344 is fabricated structural metal products), and four digits indicate fairly specific industries (e.g., 3442 is metal doors, sash frames, moldings, and trim). Despite the problems in classifying multiproduct companies, this system provides a useful basis for segmenting markets, especially for assessing market potential (see Chapter 6). For a sample of segmenting variables used in Europe for both consumer and industrial goods, see Figure 5–4.

What They Buy

What the customers do falls into two basic groupings: what they purchase in the product category, and what they do with it. Concerning what they purchase within the product category, the two major variables are the amount (usage rate) of the category and which brands/products/services are purchased. For many consumer goods, panel or similar data are available that contain purchase histories (e.g., brands purchased were A, A, A, B, A, A, C, A, A, A) on individual consumers. Such data can be analyzed by a

FIGURE 5–4

Key Segmentation Variables Used in Direct-Marketing Campaigns in Europe

Factors	Belgium	Denmark	France	Germany	Greece	Ireland	Italy	Netherlands	Portugal	Spain	United Kingdom
Most commonly used consumer segmentation criteria	Social class Nielsen zones Geographic Database	Demographic from census Database	Socio-demographic Database	Age Profession Income Family status Lifestyle	Urban/rural Profession Database	Age Income Profession Family status Database	Age Sex Profession Housing types	Age Sex Geographic Lifestyle Database	Income Urban/rural Education Political bias Database	Age Sex Education Urban/rural Geographic proximity Database	Age Sex Profession Lifestyle Database
Most commonly used business segmentation criteria	SIC* Size VAT	SIC Size Turnover Decision	SIC Size Turnover	SIC Turnover Size	Size Turnover SIC	Size Turnover Location Liquidity	SIC Size Turnover Number of telephone lines	Size/SIC Turnover Branches Credit rating Decision makers	Size SIC	Size Turnover	SIC Size

* SIC: Standard Industrial Classification

Source: *Marketing Director International.*

variety of means to measure competitive patterns (e.g., percent of switching from A to B, see Chapter 2).

For industrial and consumer goods, analysis of what (competing) product they currently use provides a basis for segmentation for new products. For example, a new plastic may be useful for replacing zinc, aluminum, brass, and so on. For Federal Express, this might consist of customers of Emery, Purolator, UPS, the U.S. Postal Service, facsimile (FAX), and so forth. Defining customers in terms of the product currently used can also lead to delineation of untapped customer segments.

Another way of looking at the "what" question is to see what customers are doing with the product. One basic set of distinctions is:

- Customer/final users.
- Industrial customers—incorporate your product in one or more products they make, includes those who manufacture and then try to sell the products and those who produce to specifications (e.g., contractors).
- Resellers—simply mark up and resell your product, perhaps with a little packaging.

In addition, defining the usage situation is crucial to understanding customers. This definition includes both where they use it (e.g., at home or in the office) and how they use it, which may or may not be related to why they originally bought it (e.g., a computer may have been bought to do book-keeping but end up acting as a word processor or, not infrequently, as decorative furniture). Products often are used in ways other than the original intent of either seller or buyer or both. It is also useful to consider "how else" customers might use the product in order to uncover new market opportunities. This would also aid in determining possible generic competitors (see Chapter 2).

Where They Buy

Purchase location is also a very important basis for analysis. Where they actually make the purchase (e.g., at home, at the office, by mail, by two-way cable TV, in a particular type of store, and so on) tends to change over time. New products are generally first purchased through specialty outlets, but as the products become better known they tend to be purchased more often through mass merchandisers. One truism is that products initially bought at high-margin specialty stores often end up as blue-light specials at Kmart (which explains the success of office supply stores such as Office Depot and Staples).

When They Buy

When they buy encompasses time of year, time of month, and even, potentially, time of day. Fast-food operators, for example, are known to segment by "daypart," that is, breakfast, lunch, dinner, and even "snacking" times. "When" can also include when they buy in terms of sales or price breaks and rebates on the assumption that those who buy on a deal may be different from those who pay full price. The increased use of promotions (both trade and consumer) by package goods manufacturers has led to the majority of many products being sold "on deal" rather than at the regular price.

How They Choose

The process by which customers buy can and should be described in several ways. First, the people involved, both formally and informally, should be identified. This means identifying the members of the buying center in industrial markets and members of the family in consumer purchase decisions who can impact the decision. Impact can take many forms, such as informational, veto power, or authorization—if I don't sign the check, we don't buy it—and all are worth delineating.

For completeness, we can specify five buying roles applicable to both consumer and industrial product purchasing decisions:

1. Initiator (identifies the need for the product).
2. Influencer (has informational or preference input to the decision).
3. Decider (makes the final decision through budget authorization).
4. Purchaser (makes the actual purchase).
5. User.

As indicated previously, the same person or different persons could potentially occupy each role. Also, a single individual often proceeds through buying stages corresponding to these roles (i.e., need identification, information search and integration, shopping, purchase, and use). Marketing managers should be aware of who occupies which role(s) and/or at what stage potential customers are.

It is also useful to describe customers in terms of the procedure they follow in making the selection. This includes not just the "rational" method in which specific benefits are considered but, more broadly, whether much deliberation is involved at all. Many purchases, though perhaps once based on careful consideration, are essentially *habitual* ("It's worked before, so . . ."), *indifference* ("They are all the same, so . . ."), or *trial* ("Looks like it's interesting, so . . .") (O'Shaughnessy, 1984). Segmenting customers into the approach followed can provide useful insights into a market.

Customers who are still considering alternatives can be described in terms of the procedure followed: extensive problem solving, limited problem solving, or routinized (Howard, 1977). In extensive problem solving (EPS), customers are concerned mainly with understanding how the product works, what it competes with, and how they would use it. EPS is generally found among first-time purchasers and products that are technologically new (e.g., 32-bit microprocessors, xerography). Limited problem solving occurs when the customer understands the basic functioning of the product and what it competes with and is concerned with evaluating the brand on a small number of attributes, typically in comparison to alternatives. This is generally the approach to most large-ticket purchases (e.g., a new piece of capital equipment).

The third basic type of purchase is routinized. In this stage, consumers essentially follow a predetermined rule for making decisions (e.g., "If we need a new typewriter, call IBM"; "If my car breaks down, call my friendly mechanic"; "If it's 10:30 break time, buy a Coke, unless Pepsi is 10 cents cheaper, in which case buy a Pepsi"). Most routine reorder purchases fall into this category, but so do many big-ticket items ("I always buy a new appliance from my local GE dealer"). Since customers following this approach can be expected to ignore most information because they have already reached a decision (usually reinforced by satisfaction with past use), the implications for marketing strategy are dramatic. For a winning product bought routinely, make it easy for the customer to keep buying and advertise "The Real Thing" (Coke), "The System Is the Solution" (AT&T), and so forth. If your product doesn't have much market share and you want to increase it, then you must "shock" the customer into considering your product either by urging variety seeking, as with "The Uncola" (7UP), or by promotions or price breaks, the ultimate of which is a free sample.

Another useful distinction in how customers buy is among planned, routine, impulse, and emergency purchases. One would expect a different buying process in the case of an emergency replacement, whether it be a toilet seat in a house or a generator in a manufacturing plant. Keeping track of the fraction of purchases of each type is a useful analysis in many circumstances.

A final way to describe how customers buy is in terms of information sources used. For example, consumer durables buyers may consult *Consumer Reports,* talk to salespeople, get recommendations from friends, examine the product in stores, and/or observe (and emulate) the behavior of experts. If, for instance, a large number emulate experts or opinion leaders (e.g., sneakers), then a strategy that is directed at key influentials may be quite successful (e.g., Nike's Air Jordan).

Why They Prefer a Product: Customer Value

Assuming customers are at least thinking about a choice (as in limited problem solving), then it is useful to understand the basis of customer value. It is important to note that we are talking about total value and not just product preferences. Choice does not equal preference; a number of factors such as convenience and company policy ("We always buy from ABC Supplies, since it is owned by my cousin") may add value to the product so choice is not fully explainable on the basis of product preference.

The concept of customer value is simple: customer value is what a product is worth to the customer. As such, it depends on the benefits offered (from the customer's point of view) and costs involved (price, hassle in purchasing, etc.). The concept of value is very different from cost: an item costing only pennies to produce may be worth thousands of dollars if it solves an important problem in a timely and efficient manner, and an expensive to produce product may have little value. Knowing the value customers place on a product makes it much easier to make various key decisions (such as setting price). A thorough discussion of customer value would require a course in consumer behavior, a large dose of marketing research, and a fairly extensive discussion of pricing. Given constraints (e.g., limited pages and the patience of both the author and the reader), what follows is a brief overview of some essential points.

The customer value of a brand is composed of three basic elements:

1. Importance of the usage situation.
2. Effectiveness of the product category in the situation.
3. Relative effectiveness of the brand in the situation.

Thus, customer value involves two basic notions of value: *absolute* value, which essentially assumes no competing brand exists (points 1 and 2 above), and *relative* value, which involves comparison of the brand with other brands. Since new markets eventually attract competitors, it is the relative effectiveness of a brand that determines its eventual share and profitability. Put differently, customer value encompasses both same form (brand) and different product category competitors, so it is important to determine not only the usage situations for which the product category has value, but also how various competitive products compare (i.e., most chemical product categories in which brand formulations vary eventually are chosen based on physical properties such as rigidity and stability under different temperatures).

Sources of Customer Value
While knowing the total value of a brand is useful for both entry/exit and pricing decisions, understanding the components of the product that

produce its value is also important. The idea that a product is a bundle of characteristics and that each characteristic has value is widely recognized (Fishbein, 1967; Lancaster, 1966; Rosenberg, 1956). Essentially, this suggests the value of each product is the sum of its values on the characteristics that comprise it:

Overall value = Σ (Value of positions on the characteristics)

1. Functional Attributes. The most obvious source of customer value is the functional or utilitarian attributes of a product. These are the basic performance features of a product (e.g., the luggage capacity, fuel economy, and other attributes of an automobile). It is important to remember that it is the perceived (by the customer) benefits and not engineering attributes that determine customer value. Since price is primarily functional, it is included here.

• *Determining Important Attributes.*   A number of approaches exist for assessing which attributes matter:

Expert Opinion. In a well-established product category, this is likely to be very useful.

Survey Data. The attributes that produce value are often ascertained by direct ratings (e.g., "How important is X?"). Importance ratings generally have two problems: Everything tends to be rated as important (and, therefore, relative importance is the key), and socially desirable answers are given (nutrition is important, and so on). Key dimensions often can be uncovered by indirect methods such as multidimensional scaling of similarity ratings (which the subject can produce without exposing his or her "biases") or by the less elegant but effective tool of focus groups.

Analysis of Buying Patterns. One measure of the importance of a characteristic is customers' resistance to giving it up. Therefore, characteristics a customer does not switch on (e.g., diet versus nondiet soft drinks) are considered important. By examining switching across products, it is possible to create a geometric model in which pairs of brands between which there is substantial switching are close together, and those pairs between which there is little switching are far apart. The identity of the dimensions of this space are interpreted as the key characteristics.

• *Establishing Positions on Attributes.*   Similarly, different approaches can be used to establish positions on attributes.

Expert Opinion. These are useful but often wrong because they tend to be based on engineering specifications rather than customer perceptions.

Survey Data. Both direct ratings ("How much of characteristic X does Product Y have?") and similarity-based positionings derived via multi-dimensional scaling are used.

2. Service. The quality of some products made in the United States has been criticized. This criticism encompasses two main thrusts: the functional attributes are at low levels and unreliable, and the other aspects of the offering, specifically service, have been neglected. Service can be broken into three categories. Before-sales service has to do with providing information. Time-of-sales service involves various aids to purchase such as reliable and fast delivery, installation and startup, and convenient financial terms. After-sales service includes both routine and emergency maintenance. Nothing is more likely to cement a long-term customer relationship than speedy and effective reaction to a problem (e.g., replacement within hours with an apology) nor to destroy one than a slow and bureaucratic one ("I'm not sure it's covered in the warranty, you must not be using it correctly, and we can't get to it for two to three weeks anyway"). Monitoring service quality has (appropriately) become much more important.

3. Image. A third source of value is the image of a product. This includes how the product "feels" (e.g., sporty, like what I had as a child, practical, luxurious) and whether that feeling matches the image the consumer wants to project. Price is clearly part of the image of a product and some customers may prefer a high price (either because they view price as a signal of quality or to engage in conspicuous consumption) while others prefer a low price. The importance of image (as opposed to functional attributes) was highlighted by the adverse reaction to the formula change made by Coke (even though it was preferred in blind taste tests) and the strong positive reaction to the reintroduction of "Classic" Coca-Cola.

4. Brand Equity. Recently, partly inspired by a wave of takeovers, the value of the brand name per se has received much attention. Brand equity is the value of a product to a consumer *beyond* that explainable by functional and service attributes, and it includes a brand's image. Brand equity can be represented by the premium a customer would pay for one brand over another when the functional and service attributes are identical. Currently, considerable effort is going into measuring brand equity, managing it (Farquhar, 1989), and seeing how well it transfers across categories, including the impact of brand extensions on the original brand (Aaker and Keller, 1990).

Brand equity derives from several sources (c.f., Aaker, 1991):

• *Awareness.* The simplest form of brand equity is familiarity. A familiar brand gives the customer a feeling of *confidence* (risk-reduction) and hence is more likely to be both considered and chosen. Evidence also shows that, on average, customers *like* brands better with which they are familiar. Finally, choosing a brand that is known gives the customer a *justification* for the decision, an explanation for his or her actions. This justification also serves a *social* role, indicating the person has bought something of value (i.e., in the case of a gift).

• *Quality Associations.* A known brand often conveys an aura of quality (either good or bad). This quality can be of the *general* halo type—"We know XYZ Company is a classy outfit that just does things right." The quality can also be *attribute or category specific*—ABC Company makes fine quality writing instruments, DEF Corporation produces user-friendly products, and GH Inc.'s products last forever (the point of the lonely Maytag repairman ads).

• *Other Associations (Brand Personality/Image).* While quality relates to product attribute associations, other more subjective and emotional associations also are an important part of brand value. These include *personal* associations; Gatorade's "Be like Mike" campaign is a blatant example of this, but every celebrity endorsement contains elements of it. Other associations are more emotional, relating to such characteristics as *stability* (see Kodak ads as well as Prudential's "A piece of the rock"), *being "hip"/"with it"* (a standard appeal of fashionable clothing companies as well as beverages and cameras as in Andre Agassi's "Image is Everything" ads), and being *responsible* (e.g., environmentally conscious, currently both an important issue and the subject of much type and posturing). Taken together, these associations form a *brand personality* that suggests for what situations a brand is (and is not) suitable (c.f., Batra, Lehmann, and Singh, 1991).

• *Loyalty.* In some sense, the strongest measure of a brand's value is the loyalty (repeat buying, word of mouth) it engenders among customers. Sometimes the loyalty is *circumstantial;* repeat buying often comes from the lack of reasonable alternatives. This includes what Aaker (1991) calls proprietary assets (e.g., patents, copyrights, trademarks) that give a firm at least a temporary monopoly position. (The impact of generic drugs when an ethical drug comes off patent suggests that much of the advantage is circumstantial and hence temporary.) Other times loyalty reflects an *efficiency* motive; the brand is good so we automatically select it to minimize effort. An important special case of this is when a customer relies on an "expert" to make the choice (e.g., a dealer) and the expert has a preferred alternative. In this case, the loyalty is really *channel-created* loyalty. Finally, the strongest form of loyalty is *attachment*. Here the customer doggedly seeks out a product, often out of deference to its role in a previous situation (i.e., "They were there when I needed them"), sometimes in an almost ritualistic manner (i.e., stopping at a certain ice cream store as a rite of summer).

Manifestations of Customer Value

A variety of signs of product value are evident:

- *Price*. Price is the company's assessment of the product's value.
- *Price sensitivity*. A product whose sales stay constant when prices increase generally is of greater value than the price.
- *Complaints and compliments*. The number of complaints and/or compliments received by the company indicates the product's value.
- *Word of mouth*. Although hard to measure, word-of-mouth comments provide a useful subjective assessment of a product's value.
- *Margin/profit contribution*. Generally higher margins indicate semi-monopoly positions and, therefore, higher relative value.
- *Dollar sales*. Total dollar sales provide an aggregate measure of the value of a product as assessed by the market.
- *Competitive activity*. Competitive activity such as new product introductions indicates the gap between customer value and company costs is large enough to allow for profits even when more companies divide the difference.
- *Repeat purchase rate*. High loyalty indicates high brand value.

Assessing the Value of the Product Category

Many ways can be devised to estimate the value of a product category. The method presented here is basically an armchair/think-about-it approach that requires the following four steps:

1. *Determining the uses*. Determine the present and potential uses to which a particular product category may be put (see the Chapter 2 discussion on determining generic competitors). This is usually done by a combination of logical analysis (e.g., asking people involved with the product or a "creative" individual what the product can do) plus customer data in the form of surveys of present users or focus groups.
2. *Estimating the importance of the uses*. In addition to introspection, survey methods that either directly ask the importance question ("On a scale of 1 to 10, how important are the following?") or

attempt to get at importance indirectly (e.g., "If a user of this product found that it failed to operate properly, how badly would he be affected?") are often used. Another useful measure of importance is the total sales potential of products that serve this use.

3. *Listing the competing product categories,* both the present and potential that service each of the uses. Competitive products can be determined from published sources, sales records, salespeople, introspection, or surveys that ask questions such as "How appropriate/useful is X as a replacement for Y?"

4. *Determining the relative effectiveness of the product category in each usage situation.* Besides introspection and expert opinion, a survey can address this by asking either, "How effective is X?" or "How much better is X than Y?"

The value of the product category (VPC) is then indicated by the sum over all uses of the importance of the use times the relative effectiveness of the product category:

$$\text{VPC} = \sum_{all\ uses} (\text{Importance}) \times (\text{Relative effectiveness})$$

More important than the total VPC, however, is the relative effectiveness of the product category for each usage situation, since these generally define separate markets.

An example of this approach, based on the microcomputer industry, appears as Figure 5–5. Rather than using numbers on a scale (e.g., rating

FIGURE 5–5

Microcomputer Product Category Value Estimation (Random Customer #007)

Use	(IMP) Importance	Competitive Products	(REL) Relative Effectiveness	Category Value (IMP) × (REL)
Video games	Some 20	TV attachments, board games	Very good	High
Bookkeeping	None 1	Accountant, service bureau, "books"	Marginal	Low
Learning skills	Very low 4	Books, school	Inferior	Low
Data analysis	Large 65	Large-scale computer, time sharing, consultant, calculator	Good	High
Report preparation	A little 10 — 100	Typewriter, word processor, secretarial service	Good	Moderate

relative effectiveness from 1 to 10), this example used adjectives. A numerical system is better, but only after analyzing enough product categories to know which numbers are good/big and which are not. From Figure 5–5 it should be noted that (1) it is fairly easy to structure the table, (2) some of the entries will be hard to quantify, and (3) limited confidence is likely to exist in many of the entries. Quantifying the entries is a problem if one desires a precise estimate of the value. Still, even such entries as "not very effective" can provide guidance as to the product's value. Regarding the limited confidence in some of the entries, the appropriate procedure is to vary each of the entries and see if it matters. If the value is sensitive to relatively small variations, this suggests an area where more precise research is needed.

Assessing the Value of the Brand/Product/Service

Assessing the total value of a brand can be done indirectly. A high-value brand has: high share, high repeat purchase rate, low elasticity with respect to price, and limited competitive brand shopping.

Using customer responses to estimate the value of a product generally involves direct ratings of the brand. This includes several different approaches:

1. *Direct ratings* on a scale (e.g., "How good is X for use Y?") for all competing products and then a comparison. Remember we are generally interested in relative and not absolute value. Therefore, an average of 4 on a 5-point scale indicates good values if the other products are getting 2s and 3s, but little value if the other products are getting averages of 4.5 and 4.8.
2. *Constant sum ratings across brands,* such as "Please rate the following four brands in terms of how well they work in use by dividing 10 points among them:"

Brand A	————
Brand B	————
Brand C	————
Brand D	————
Total	10

3. *Graded paired comparisons* require customers to indicate which of a pair of products is preferred and by how much. This is often done in terms of dollar amounts (Pessemier, 1963), as shown in Figure 5–6.
4. *Conjoint analysis* is a procedure whereby customers rate products described in terms of attributes, price, and brand name. Through

analysis (basically regression analysis), the relative importance of the attributes, price, and brand name are determined.

As an example of conjoint analysis, assume there are three important attributes in a notebook computer purchase decision: weight, battery life, and brand. The product manager would like to determine the relative importance of the three attributes before making product development and communications decisions. Assume also that each characteristic can have two different levels or values as shown in Figure 5–7. An analyst might wish to understand which attributes are valued and, perhaps more important, which attributes have relatively greater impact on preference. A study can be designed where the respondent's task is to rank order the eight combinations from most preferred to least preferred.

In Figure 5–7, a hypothetical response to the rank-ordering task gives a 1 to the most preferred combination and an 8 to the least preferred. One combination (6 pounds, 4 hours, Compaq) clearly dominates and another (10 pounds, 2 hours, Gateway) is clearly the worst. However, trade-offs

FIGURE 5–6
Dollar Metric Example: Soft Drink Preference

Pair of Brands (more preferred brand circled)	Amount Extra Willing to Pay to Get a Six-Pack of the More Preferred Brand (cents)
Data	
(Coke) Pepsi	2
(Coke) 7UP	8
(Coke) Dr Pepper	5
(Coke) Fresca	12
(Pepsi) 7UP	6
(Pepsi) Dr Pepper	3
(Pepsi) Fresca	10
7UP (Dr Pepper)	3
(7UP) Fresca	4
(Dr Pepper) Fresca	7

Analysis

Coke:	+ 2 (versus Pepsi) + 8 (versus 7UP) + 5 (versus Dr Pepper) + 12 (versus Fresca)	=	27
Pepsi:	− 2 + 6 + 3 + 10	=	17
7UP:	− 8 − 6 − 3 + 4	=	− 13
Dr Pepper:	− 5 − 3 + 3 + 7	=	2
Fresca:	− 12 − 10 − 4 − 7	=	− 33

must be made in between those two options. In this case, the average desirability value for the 6-pound option is 6.5 $\left(\dfrac{5 + 6 + 7 + 8}{4}\right)$, and for the 10-pound option is 2.5. Similarly, for the 4-hour option, the average value is 5.0; for the 2-hour option, 4.0; for a Compaq, 5.5; and for a Gateway, 3.5. Looking at the differences in the average ranks, the most important characteristic to this respondent is weight, followed by brand name, and finally battery life. Thus, a 6-pound Compaq with battery life of 2 hours is worth more than a 6-pound Gateway with 6-hour battery life (6.5 + 4.0 + 5.5 = 16 versus 6.5 + 5.0 + 3.5 = 15). On the other hand, a 10-pound Compaq with 2 hours of battery life is not worth as much as a 6-pound Gateway with a 2-hour life (2.5 + 4.0 + 5.5 = 12.0 versus 6.5 + 4.0 + 3.5 = 14.0). Here brand name (equity) is more crucial than battery life but not enough to make up for being too heavy.

FIGURE 5–7

Hypothetical Conjoint Analysis: Notebook Computers

I. Attributes and levels to study
    Weight (6 pounds or 10 pounds)
    Battery life (2 hours or 4 hours)
    Brand name (Gateway or Compaq)
II. Respondent task: Rank order all combinations of these characteristics.
III. Input data

Computer	Respondent Ranking	Derived Desirability (9 ranking)
6 pounds, 2 hours, Gateway	4	5
10 pounds, 4 hours, Compaq	5	4
10 pounds, 2 hours, Gateway	8	1
6 pounds, 4 hours, Gateway	3	6
6 pounds, 2 hours, Compaq	2	7
10 pounds, 4 hours, Gateway	7	2
10 pounds, 2 hours, Compaq	6	3
6 pounds, 4 hours, Compaq	1	8

IV. Analysis

	Average Desirability	Difference
Weight:		
6 pounds	6.5	
10 pounds	2.5	4.0
Battery life:		
2 hours	4.0	
4 hours	5.0	1.0
Brand:		
Gateway	3.5	
Compaq	5.5	2.0

While the actual design and analysis of conjoint studies are more complicated than that shown (the design includes selection of attributes, the number and specific levels for each attribute, and the particular combinations to be shown respondents to trade off between information needs and respondent fatigue), the basic ideas are the same. This analysis can be done at the individual or aggregate level, but is typically more useful if done separately for different market segments. For a more detailed description of this technique, see Lehmann (1989).

Will They Buy It (Again)?

Quality/Satisfaction
Perhaps the most obvious trend in business in the late 1980s and early 1990s has been the zeal with which quality programs have been promoted, especially in the United States. Actually, providing quality in order to satisfy customers and retain them as future customers is simply a restatement of the basic principle of marketing (i.e., to create and maintain customers). Similarly, so-called relationship marketing also stresses the long-term value of a customer where a single transaction (i.e., a sale) is not the ultimate goal.

Quality is ultimately measured in terms of customer satisfaction. Further, satisfaction has a strong relative component to it. (Are customers of a certain product category more or less satisfied than those of a different but potentially substitutable one? Are customers of my company's product more or less satisfied than customers of a competitor's?)

The direct measurement of satisfaction has evolved to consider several aspects:

1. Expectations of performance/quality.
2. Perceived performance/quality.
3. The gap between expectations and performance.

Much of the early work focused on the gap between expectations and performance, and a widely used scale, called SERVQUAL (Parasuraman, Zeithaml, and Berry, 1988), has been developed based on it. Recently, however, the direct impact of expectations and performance on satisfaction has been emphasized as well as the effect of expectations on perceived performance (Anderson and Sullivan, 1993; Boulding, Staelin, Kalra, and Zeithaml, 1992). Thus, satisfaction is now typically modeled as a function of expectations, performance, and the difference between expectations and performance (with "negative disconfirmation," when performance falls short of expectations, having a much stronger impact than positive disconfirmation).

In assessing satisfaction, it is important to compare satisfaction with your own company with that of other companies in the industry/category and other companies in general, especially those in categories that are potential substitutes. Several authors have begun to assemble satisfaction data across industries (see Fornell, 1992). Comparability of measures is crucial if satisfaction results are to be maximally useful.

Indirect measures of satisfaction abound. These include word-of-mouth comments, complaints, and perhaps most importantly repeat purchase (or lack thereof). The basic reason for caring about satisfaction is that it leads to customer retention. Hence, measures of intended or actual repeat purchasing provide a useful way to simultaneously measure satisfaction and its impact. (It is possible for customers to be satisfied but not repurchase because of poor product supply, variety seeking/multiple sourcing, large promotional deals, and so on.)

Intentions

Intentions are imprecise predictors of future purchase (as in he/she "had good intentions but . . ."). Still, they provide early signs of future sales. Surveys of customers (asking "Would you buy _____?" on either a fixed scale such as 1–7 or a 100-point scale and/or "How much _____ will you buy?") are a staple input to sales forecasts, especially for industrial products, and we discuss them in greater detail in the forecasting chapter.

Sensitivity to Elements of the Marketing Mix

Why consumers buy also includes response to elements of the marketing mix. In addition to the product itself, sensitivity to and preference for prices (and means of payment), distribution and availability (including the effect of direct marketing), advertising, promotion, and service are fundamental aspects of a market. Moreover, sensitivity typically varies by customer, and at least a segment-level analysis is usually called for. Methods for assessing sensitivity include:

1. *Expert judgment,* using the knowledge of managers, salespeople, etc.
2. *Customer survey-based methods,* including both direct questioning (e.g., "How important is . . . ?") and more subtle approaches such as conjoint analysis.
3. *Experiments,* including both controlled settings (e.g., in shopping malls or specially designed stores) and in actual markets.
4. *Analyses of past data,* comparing results across markets, or where individual customer record data is available (e.g., scanner data) at the individual level. Such analysis often uses techniques such as

regression analysis to predict sales as a function of mix elements or logit analysis (basically a type of regression) to assess the impact of mix elements on market share or individual choice probabilities.

Assessing sensitivity to elements of the marketing mix is a large, ongoing task. The output of this assessment has implications primarily for the tactical/programmatic elements of marketing (e.g., how much to spend on advertising). Further, this assessment requires specialized data not readily available outside the company. Therefore, given our focus on the more strategic elements of marketing, we do not discuss mix assessment in detail here.

SEGMENTATION

Assuming we have described customers as in Figure 5–1, it is useful to group the customers into segments. (Of course, if there are only five customers, no grouping is required since we can treat each one separately.) It is important to recognize that segmentation is not right or wrong, but rather useful or not useful. Segments are not naturally determined (e.g., by DNA molecules) but rather are mainly a creation of the analyst/strategist to either simplify the world or to get a new perspective on it.

Selecting a Basis for Segmentation

Given the tremendous number of potential bases for segmentation, a pertinent question is: Which one to use? Actually, several can be used in combination, so the question is really: What makes a basis for segmentation a good one? While there is no single way to say what is best (anyone suggesting there is probably doesn't understand the problem or is selling a particular segmentation method), the following six criteria provide a useful standard for evaluation:

1. Sizable
Segments must be of sufficient size in terms of potential sales (but not in terms of number of customers) to be worth worrying about. (As a rule, billion dollar companies don't care much about J. R. Smith at 1188 Maple Street, or all the people on Maple Street for that matter.)

2. Identifiable
Segments should be identifiable so that when presenting results they can be referred to by more pleasing titles than segment A, segment B (e.g., the

35-to-50 segment, the sports-minded, companies in New York). The identity of the segments often provides an aid to strategic and tactical decisions.

3. Reachable
It may be sufficient for strategic purposes to identify a segment, but for planning the marketing mix (e.g., advertising), it is useful to be able to target efforts on a segment. A sports-minded segment tends to be reachable through the media (e.g., *Sports Illustrated*), whereas people who prefer the color blue, though identified, may be harder to reach efficiently (except by labels on blue towels, or by copy that employs the color blue).

4. Respond Differently
Ideally, segments should respond differently to at least some of the elements of the offering. If all segments respond the same, then no specialized programs can be used. For example, some customers may be sensitive to advertising but not price, whereas others are concerned about price but unaffected by advertising, and still others care about a single attribute such as downtime. The sensitivity to changes in market offering forms a useful basis for both describing the overall market and defining segments. It also makes the "why they buy" part of the analysis crucial.

5. Coherent
When interpreting a segment, it is implicitly assumed that all members behave in essentially the same way; that is, that segment members are homogeneous. This is always violated to some extent. What is important is that the average member of a segment be reasonably close to the rest of the members. Hence, an important conceptual requirement of a segment is that the within-segment variation in behavior be (much) smaller than the between-segment variation. (This desired condition is often operationalized as the basis for tests for determining the number of segments.)

6. Stable
Since future plans are based on past data, segments (and hopefully but not necessarily the members of those segments) should be fairly stable over time.

Methods for Deriving Segments

Data Based
These methods begin with a data set of actual or potential customers and then form groups (segments). One way of generating segments is to collect

data from a sample of customers on a series of variables and then form groups by using cluster analysis. This is sometimes called looking for natural clusters, which was the purpose of cluster analysis in fields such as biology. When one sees the mathematics involved, however, it is clear the process is anything but natural.

General Characteristics. By *general characteristics,* we mean the "who" type descriptors (demographics, firm size, etc.) described earlier. Grouping customers this way results in identifiable and reachable segments but not necessarily ones that respond very differently (e.g., in terms of brand preference or usage rates). Nonetheless, this method produces clusters that are sometimes quite interesting. One example of this is the lifestyle-based clusters used by advertising agencies in designing copy strategy.

Criterion-Related. Rather than treat all the variables as equals as in cluster analysis, this method assumes one variable is the criterion (e.g., product class usage) and then attempts to find which other variables (e.g., age, income) are most highly related to it. The market is then segmented on the basis of these variables.

A variety of statistical procedures are available for such studies, including cross-tabulation, analysis of variance, and AID. (See Figure 5–8 for a list of analytical methods used in examining customer differences.) At least for the first stages of such research, however, some form of regression analysis is frequently used. In performing such regressions, it is often useful to treat the variables as "categorical" (by using a series of so-called dummy

FIGURE 5–8
Analytical Methods for Examining Customers

Identifying relations among two variables:
    Cross-tabs (categorical variables)
    Correlations (continuous variables)

Predicting a criterion variable based on several other variables:
    ANOVA
    Regression
    Discriminant analysis
    AID (Automatic Interaction Detector)

Simplifying a database:
    Factor analysis: identifying redundant variables
    Cluster analysis: forming segments
    Multidimensional scaling: graphically representing a number of alternatives on a small
      number of dimensions

variables). These regressions (at least for frequently purchased consumer products) tend to produce poor fits with individual behavior. Yet, despite the low R-squareds, these regressions often point to useful bases for segmentation. For example, Bass, Tigert, and Lonsdale (1968) found significant differences in product category usage based on demographics such as age and income (see Figure 5–9). Similar results were found by Assael and Roscoe (1976) in segmenting the market of long-distance phone expenditures.

Another example involves grouping consumers of soft drinks based on their purchase frequencies of eight soft drinks (Bass, Pessemier, and Lehmann, 1972; Lehmann, 1976). Here 10 segments were formed (see Figure 5–10, page 115) providing an interesting view of the market in terms of brand preference, with a segment emerging as loyal to each of the three largest-selling brands: Coke, Pepsi, and 7UP.

An example of the importance of considering customer behavior rather than just customer descriptors in forming segments is provided by Rangan, Moriarty, and Swartz (1992). They segment national accounts of a large industrial company based on the trade-offs they make between price and service, and show additional insights over analysis based on such variables as size, industry, or even the stated importance of product benefits sought. Specifically they found four segments:

1. Programmed Buyers—essentially small customers who routinely bought the item and didn't consider it very important.
2. Relationship Buyers—small buyers who got lower price and higher service but were loyal to the supplier.
3. Transaction Buyers—larger buyers for whom the product was important who got price discounts and expected high service but were not loyal.
4. Bargain Hunters—large buyers who got the lowest prices and the highest service. (It may not pay to try to serve these customers since they are so demanding that they may not be profitable.)

Latent Class Methods.   The two previous methods begin with individual customers and then aggregate them. Latent class methods, by contrast, begin with the market as a whole and then determine what segmentation pattern best trades off parsimony (few segments) and the ability to explain overall behavior based on derived segments in which all customers in a segment behave identically. These are intriguing methods but require considerable sophistication to employ (see Appendix 5A).

A simple kind of latent structure analysis focuses on brand-switching data and attempts to derive segments similar to those in Figure 5–10. However, rather than estimating share at the individual level and then

FIGURE 5–9
Light and Heavy Buyers by Mean Purchase Rates for Different Socioeconomic Cells

R^2	Product	Description		Mean Consumption Rate Ranges			Ratio of Highest to Lowest Rate
		Light Buyers	Heavy Buyers	Light Buyers	Heavy Buyers		
.08	Ketchup	Unmarried or married over age 50 without children	Under 50, three or more children	.74–1.82	2.73–5.79		7.8
.07	Frozen orange juice	Under 35 or over 65, income less than $10,000, not college grads, two or less children	College grads, income over $10,000, between 35 and 65	1.12–2.24	3.53–9.00		8.0
.04	Pancake mix	Some college, two or less children	Three or more children, high school or less education	.48–.52	1.10–1.51		3.3
.08	Candy bars	Under 35, no children	35 or over, three or more children	1.01–4.31	6.56–22.29		21.9
	Cake mix	Not married or under 35, no children, income under $10,000, TV less than 3½ hours	35 or over, three or more children, income over $10,000	.55–1.10	2.22–3.80		6.9
.09	Beer	Under 25 or over 50, college education, nonprofessional, TV less than 2 hours	Between 25 and 50, not college graduate, TV more than 3½ hours	0–12.33	17.26–40.30		—
.02	Cream shampoo	Income less than $8,000, at least some college, less than five children	Income $10,000 or over with high school or less education	16–35	44–87		5.5
.06	Hair spray	Over 65, under $8,000 income	Under 65, over $10,000 income, not college graduate	0–.41	.52–1.68		—
.09	Toothpaste	Over 50, less than three children, income less than $8,000	Under 50, three or more children, over $10,000 income	1.41–2.01	2.22–4.39		3.1
.03	Mouthwash	Under 35 or over 65, less than $8,000 income, some college	Between 35 and 65, income over $8,000, high school or less education	.46–.85	.98–1.17		2.5

Source: Frank Bass, Douglas Tigert, and Ronald Lonsdale. " Market Segmentation: Group versus Individual Behavior." Reprinted from *Journal of Marketing Research*, published by the American Marketing Association 5 (August 1968). p. 267.

FIGURE 5–10
Average Purchase Probability by Brand

Segment	Percentage of Sample	Coke	7UP	Tab	Like	Pepsi	Sprite	Diet Pepsi	Fresca
1	14.0	.58	.04	.02	.06	.15	.07	.02	.07
2	13.2	.91	.03	.01	.01	.02	.01	.00	.01
3	16.5	.17	.11	.02	.04	.52	.06	.02	.06
4	10.3	.06	.74	.01	.03	.03	.10	.01	.02
5	3.7	.07	.11	.00	.01	.10	.64	.00	.06
6	6.6	.08	.04	.11	.16	.12	.02	.40	.07
7	8.6	.10	.25	.08	.16	.08	.17	.05	.11
8	11.9	.06	.03	.00	.00	.86	.04	.00	.01
9	11.1	.40	.30	.02	.04	.11	.07	.01	.05
10	4.1	.11	.06	.04	.09	.10	.10	.02	.48

Source: Donald R. Lehmann, "An Empirically Based Stochastic Model," *Journal of Business Research* 4, no. 4 (November 1976), p. 352.

grouping (e.g., via cluster analysis) similar individuals together, this method simply derives segment level probabilities and market shares. Grover and Srinivasan (1987) provide an example of such segmentation for the instant-coffee market. Subjects who always bought the same brand were classified as loyals while the rest (switchers) were then broken into various numbers of segments. The four-segment solution, which appeared to be the best compromise between explanation and parsimony, appears as Figure 5–11. The results suggest very small hard-core loyal segments (which account for 35 percent of the market) and four switching segments with tendencies to favor two or more brands.

Kamakura and Russell (1989) extend this approach to include price sensitivity. They analyze 78 weeks of purchases of a refrigerated (once opened) food product with a 10-week average purchase cycle. The four brands (A, B, C, P) were average priced at $4.29, $3.54, $3.38, and $3.09 and had choice shares of 35.8, 27.8, 23.8, and 12.6 percent, respectively. The resulting segments appear in Figure 5–12. Interestingly, these results also suggest about one third (31.4 percent) of the customers are hard-core loyal. In addition, the segments differ in terms of price sensitivity. Segments one and two, which account for 19 percent of the market, appear to be relatively insensitive to price and fairly brand loyal. By contrast, segments three and four, which account for 42.2 percent of the market, are quite price sensitive and tend to spread purchases across several brands. Segment five appears not to respond to price or be very brand loyal; perhaps this (small, 7.4 percent) segment represents customers for whom the product is low involvement and who simply "pick" a brand by reaching for the most readily available one.

FIGURE 5–11
Four-Segment Solution for the Instant-Coffee Market

Brand[a,b,c]			Manufacturer[d]	Aggregate Market Share (MS)	Brand Loyal Weight (V)	Switching Segments			
						Weights W (total = .65)			
						1 .19*	2 .22*	3 .18*	4 .06*
						Within-Segment Market Shares ($\hat{p}$)[e]			
HP	D	R	PG	.13	.05*	.09*	.20*	.13*	.08
TC	C	FD	N	.10	.04*	.07*	.03	.18*	.03
TC	D	FD	N	.07	.01	—[f]	—	.32*	.12*
FL	C	R	PG	.12	.04*	.20*	.16*	.04*	—
MH	C	R	GF	.21	.08*	.42*	.15*	.07*	.06
S	D	R	GF	.16	.07*	.04	.22*	.11*	.15*
S	D	FD	GF	.03	.01*	—	.05*	.03*	—
MX	C	FD	GF	.04	.01*	.04*	.03*	.04*	—
N	C	R	N	.06	.01*	.14*	—	—	.27*
N	D	R	N	.03	.01	—	.07*	—	.27*
B	D	FD	GF	.05	.02*	—	.09*	.08*	.02
Totals				1.00	1.00[g]	1.00	1.00	1.00	1.00

* Parameter estimate/standard error > 2.
[a] Brand names: HP = High Point, TC = Taster's Choice, FL = Folgers, MH = Maxwell House, S = Sanka, MX = Maxim, N = Nescafé, B = Brim.
[b] D = decaffeinated, C = caffeinated.
[c] FD = freeze dried, R = regular (spray dried).
[d] PG = Procter & Gamble, GF = General Foods, N = Nestlé.
[e] Underlined numbers denote the two largest choice probabilities within the segment.
[f] Probabilities constrained to zero for model identification.
[g] Total includes the total weight of switching segments (= .65).

Source: Rajiv Grover and V. Srinivasan, "A Simultaneous Approach to Market Segmentation and Market Structuring," Journal of Marketing Research 24 (May 1987), p. 147.

FIGURE 5–12

Preference Segmentation and Price Sensitivity

	Loyal Segments				Switching Segments*				
	A	B	C	P	1	2	3	4	5
Choice probabilities									
A	1				.790	.219	.152	.095	.192
B		1			.089	.646	.259	.238	.332
C			1		.069	.092	.520	.301	.133
P				1	.052	.043	.065	.367	.343
Segment size (% of all households)									
	19.0	5.8	3.9	2.7	9.3	9.7	25.8	16.4	7.4
Price sensitivity									
β					−1.87	−1.44	−3.07	−5.42	.37 †

* For switching segments 1 through 4, purchase probabilities greater than .10 are underlined.
† Price coefficient statistically *insignificant* at the .05 level.

Source: Wagner A. Kamakura and Gary J. Russell, "A Probabilistic Choice Model for Market Segmentation and Elasticity Structure," *Journal of Marketing Research* 26 (November 1989), p. 385.

A Priori

There is a strong tendency to want to derive segments by examining data. Still, some of the most useful segmentation schemes are on such bases as customer usage rate (heavy users, light users, nonusers) or product preference. While these are not elegant, they are often more useful than so-called natural clusters because they are readily identifiable and reachable and obviously have responded differently to the product offering. In fact, it is always advisable to use such segmentation strategy as at least a basis for comparison with the results of more "data massaging"-oriented approaches.

No simple way exists to tell how to get the best segmentation scheme. In that respect it's a lot like art—you can tell whether you like it or not but never prove it's the best. Figure 5–13 (constructed based on intuition during an airport delay) is an example of the efficiency with which a segmentation scheme can be used to summarize a lot of customer analysis information.

SUMMARY

All of the phases of customer analysis provide potentially useful information. However, a tremendous amount of this information can be summarized in a figure that includes segments across the top and the various phases of customer analysis as the rows of the figure to describe the segments, as in Figure 5–14.

FIGURE 5–13
Segmentation of Ski Buyers

Segment	Heroes	Basic Values	Favorite Eastern U.S. Resorts	Preferred Skis and Boots	Clothing	Product	Price	Distribution	Effective Advertising
Social skiers	Suzy Chaffee	Looking good, fresh air	Convenient, intermediate (Stratton, Bromley)	Look good, easy to use	Matching outfits	Package deals	Anything reasonable	One-stop shopping, convenient, ski shops	Social
Hot non-experts	James Bond, downhill racer, Alberto Tomba	Being seen, adrenalin rush	Good lift lines, sufficient challenge (Hunter, Mount Snow)	Just below top of the line	Stylishly outlandish	Popular models	Moderate	Malls, Herman's	Self-image
Serious exercisers	Grizzly Adams, Bo Jackson	Work out, being outdoors	Challenge and variety (Pico, Cannon)	Value for the money, good to top of the line	Comfort, last year's/ decade's style	Performance, versatility, durability	Price conscious	Sales, discounters	Informational
Performance seekers	Ingemar Stenmark, Marc Girardelli	Being tested, improving	Big and steep, moguls (Stowe, Mad River)	Top of the line	Comfort, functional	Special characteristics	Will pay for quality	Pro shops	Informational

The process of arriving at a useful version of Figure 5–14 is likely to be messy and imprecise and involve trial and error. The best approach, once an attempt has been made to address the issues of Figure 5–1, is to try several schemes for defining the segments (e.g., versions of who, why, etc., possibly in combination). The choice of which segmentation scheme (described as in Figure 5–14) to use then depends on the insight gained and the potential for the segmentation scheme to lead to useful strategies (e.g., selecting which segments to serve) and efficient program (e.g., advertising, distribution) determination.

In analyzing the customer, it is only natural to look at history. Nonetheless, the reason for doing so is not to be a good historian, but to be a good forecaster. Put differently, one needs to make judgments about what

FIGURE 5–14
Basic Format for Summarizing Customer Analysis

Customer Description	Segment				
	I	II	III	IV	. . .
1. Who they are: Purchaser User					
2. What they buy: What they buy: amount What they buy: brand, features What they do with it: usage situation					
3. Where they buy.					
4. When they buy: Time of year, month, week, day On sale/promotion versus full price					
5. How they choose: Decision participants' roles Process Information sources; shopping locations					
6. Why they select a product: customer value: Functional attributes Service Image Brand equity					
7. Will they buy it (again)? Satisfaction Intention					
8. Sensitivity to mix: Product Price Distribution Advertising Promotion Service					

might cause behavior to change (both your actions and outside influences: culture, competition, economic conditions, regulation, and so on). In addition, some assessment is needed of the likelihood these "causal" influences will change. Finally, the impact of the likely or reasonable changes on customer behavior, and consequently sales, must be analyzed. Then and only then will customer analysis be useful for deciding what you will do in the future and what trends you will monitor most closely.

APPENDIX: LATENT CLASS METHODS

Recent advances in both computer power and methods have made feasible a different approach to segment construction and interpretation. Most methods discussed in the chapter basically attempt to take individuals and collect/aggregate them into segments. By contrast, latent class methods simultaneously estimate segment sizes and their behavior. These methods use the simple fact that aggregate market behavior is the sum of individual or segment level behavior:

$$\text{Total Market Behavior} = \sum_{segments} \left(\begin{array}{c} \text{Size of} \\ \text{Segment } i \end{array} \right) \left(\begin{array}{c} \text{Behavior of} \\ \text{Segment } i \end{array} \right)$$

$$= \sum_{segments} w_i \, B_i$$

The latent class approach *simultaneously* estimates segment sizes (w_s) and segment behavior (B_s). Segment membership is not known in advance (i.e., there is not a high-income or nonresponsive-to-promotion segment specified in advance) and individual customers are not "assigned to" particular segments.

A key issue involves deciding on the number of segments. Basically, this decision involves trading off between better describing a market (which allowing for more segments always does because it increases the number of parameters estimated) and keeping only important/"significant" segments. This trade-off is often accomplished with statistical tests on results of allowing for an additional segment (e.g., five versus four segments) or by comparing the abilities of the more and less parsimonious models to forecast behavior of a "holdout" sample (that is, customers who were not used to estimate the parameters).

When there are enough data to estimate behavior at the individual customer level, latent class methods often incorporate probabilities of segment membership for each customer:

$$\text{Market behavior} = \sum_{customers} \sum_{segments} P_{ij} \, B_i$$

where P_{ij} = probability person j is a member of segment i

In interpreting such analyses, it is desirable to describe segments in terms of descriptor variables (demographics, firm characteristics). This can be done separately from the latent class analysis by relating individuals' estimated probabilities of being in each segment to other characteristics; (that is, letting $P_{ij} = f$ (characteristics of customer j). This two-step approach then becomes:

$$\text{Step 1: Market behavior} = \sum_{customers} \sum_{segments} P_{ij} B_i$$

$$\text{Step 2: } P_{ij} = \sum_{characteristics} C_{\ell_i} X_{\ell_j}$$

Occasionally, the two steps are combined in a single step:

$$\text{Market behavior} = \sum_{customers} \sum_{segments} \sum_{\substack{charac- \\ teristics}} (C_{\ell_i} X_{\ell_j} B_i)$$

Currently, latent class methods have not been widely applied in commercial settings. It is a good bet, however, that their use will increase substantially.

REFERENCES

Aaker, David A. *Managing Brand Equity*. New York: Free Press, 1991.

Aaker, David A., and Kevin Lane Keller. "Consumer Evaluations of Brand Extensions." *Journal of Marketing* 54, (January 1990), pp. 27–41.

Anderson, Eugene W., and Mary W. Sullivan. "The Antecedents and Consequences of Customer Satisfaction for Firms." *Marketing Science,* 12, (Spring 1993), pp. 125–43.

Assael, Henry, and A. Marvin Roscoe, Jr. "Approaches to Market Segmentation Analysis." *Journal of Marketing* 40, (October 1976), pp. 67–76.

Barabba, Vincent, and Gerald Zaltman. *Hearing the Voice of the Market*. New York: McGraw-Hill, 1991.

Bass, Frank M.; Edgar A. Pessemier; and Donald R. Lehmann. "An Experimental Study of Relationships between Attitudes, Brand Preference, and Choice." *Behavioral Science* 17, (November 1972), pp. 532–41.

Bass, Frank M.; Douglas J. Tigert, Jr.; and Ronald T. Lonsdale. "Market Segmentation—Group versus Individual Behavior." *Journal of Marketing Research* 5, (August 1968), pp. 264–70.

Batra, Rajeev; Donald R. Lehmann; and Dipinder Singh. "The Brand Personality Component of Brand Goodwill: Some Antecedents and Consequences." In David A. Aaker and Alexander L. Biel, eds., *Brand Equity and Advertising: Advertising's Role in Building Strong Brands,* Hillsdale, N.J.: Lawrence Erlbaum Associates, Inc., 1993.

Belk, Russell W. "Situational Variables and Consumer Behavior." *Journal of Consumer Research* 2, (December 1975), pp. 157–64.

Boulding, William; Richard Staelin; Ajay Kalra; and Valerie A. Zeithaml. "Conceptualizing and Testing a Dynamic Process Model of Service Quality." Cambridge, Mass.: Marketing Science Institute Working Paper, 1992, pp. 92–127.

Corfman, Kim P.; Donald R. Lehmann; and Sundar Narayanan. "Values, Utility, and Ownership: Modeling the Relationships for Consumer Durables." *Journal of Retailing* 67, (Summer 1991), pp. 184–204.

Cravens, David W.; Gerald E. Hills; and Robert B. Woodruff. *Marketing Decision Making: Concepts and Strategy,* rev. ed. Homewood, Ill.: Richard D. Irwin, 1980.

Day, George S. *Strategic Marketing Planning.* St. Paul, Minn.: West Publishing Co., 1984.

Doyle, Peter, and John Saunders. "Market Segmentation and Positioning in Specialized Industrial Markets." *Journal of Marketing* 49, (Spring 1985), pp. 24–32.

Farquhar, Peter H. "Managing Brand Equity." *Marketing Research,* September 1989, pp. 28–33.

Ferber, Robert, ed. *Handbook of Marketing Research.* New York: McGraw-Hill, 1974.

Fishbein, Martin. "Attitudes and the Prediction of Behavior." In *Readings in Attitude Theory and Measurement.* Ed. Martin Fishbein. New York: John Wiley & Sons, 1967, pp. 477–92.

Fornell, Claes. "A National Customer Satisfaction Barometer: The Swedish Experience." *Journal of Marketing* 56, (January 1992), pp. 6–21.

Frank, Ronald E.; William F. Massy; and Yoram Wind. *Market Segmentation.* Englewood Cliffs, N.J.: Prentice Hall, 1972.

Green, Paul E., and Wayne S. DeSarbo. "Componential Segmentation in the Analysis of Consumer Trade-Offs." *Journal of Marketing* 43, (Fall 1979), pp. 83–91.

Grover, Rajiv, and V. Srinivasan. "Evaluating the Multiple Effects of Retail Promotions on Brand Loyal and Brand Switching Segments." *Journal of Marketing Research* 29, (February 1992), pp. 76–89.

Grover, Rajiv, and V. Srinivasan. "A Simultaneous Approach to Market Segmentation and Market Structuring." *Journal of Marketing Research* 24, (May 1987), pp. 139–52.

Howard, John A. *Consumer Behavior: Application of Theory.* New York: McGraw-Hill, 1977.

"The IBM-DEC Wars: It's 'The Year of the Customer.'" *Business Week,* March 30, 1987, pp. 86–87.

Kahle, Lynn R.; Sharon E. Beatty; and Pamela Homer. "Alternative Measurement Approaches to Customer Values; The List of Values (LOV) and Values and Life Styles (VALS)." *Journal of Consumer Research* 13, (December 1986), pp. 405–9.

Kamakura, Wagner A., and Gary J. Russell. "A Probabilistic Choice Model for Market Segmentation and Elasticity Structure." *Journal of Marketing Research,* 26 (November 1989), pp. 379–90.

Kassarjian, Harold H. "Personality and Consumer Behavior: A Review." *Journal of Marketing Research* 8, (November 1971), pp. 409–19.

Kotler, Philip. *Marketing Management: Analysis, Planning, and Control,* 4th ed. Englewood Cliffs, N.J.: Prentice Hall, 1980.

Lancaster, Kelvin J. "A New Approach to Consumer Theory." *Journal of Political Economy* 74, (April 1966), pp. 132–57.

Lehmann, Donald R. *Market Research and Analysis,* 3rd ed. Homewood, Ill.: Richard D. Irwin, 1989.

Lehmann, Donald R. "An Empirically Based Stochastic Model." *Journal of Business Research* 4, (November 1976), pp. 3437–56.

Massy, William F.; Ronald E. Frank; and Thomas M. Lodahl. *Purchasing Behavior and Personal Attributes.* Philadelphia: University of Pennsylvania Press, 1968.

Mitchell, Arnold. *The Nine American Life Styles.* New York: Warner Books, 1983.

O'Shaughnessy, John. *Competitive Marketing: A Strategic Approach.* Winchester, Mass.: Allen & Unwin, 1984.

Parasuraman, A.; Valarie A. Zeithaml; and Leonard L. Berry. "SERVQUAL: A Multiple-Item Scale for Measuring Consumer Perceptions of Service Quality." *Journal of Retailing* 64, (Spring 1988), pp. 12–37.

Pessemier, Edgar A. *Experimental Methods of Analyzing Demand for Branded Consumer Goods with Applications to Problems in Marketing Strategy,* bulletin no. 39. Pullman, Wash.: Washington State University Bureau of Economic and Business Research, June 1963.

Rangan, V. Kasturi; Rowland T. Moriarty; and Gordon S. Swartz. "Segmenting Customers in Mature Industrial Markets." *Journal of Marketing* 56, (October 1992), pp. 72–82.

Rosenberg, M. J. "Cognitive Structure and Attitudinal Affect." *Journal of Abnormal and Social Psychology* 53, (November 1956), pp. 367–72.

Schiffman, Leon G., and Michael D. Jones. "New York Telephone's Use of VALS." *Marketing Review* 38, (December–January 1983), pp. 25–29.

Warshaw, Paul R. "A New Model for Predicting Behavioral Intentions: An Alternative to Fishbein." *Journal of Marketing Research* 17, (May 1980), pp. 153–72.

Wells, William D. "Psychographics: A Critical Review." *Journal of Marketing Research* 12, (May 1975), pp. 196–213.

Winter, Frederick W. "A Cost-Benefit Approach to Market Segmentation," *Journal of Marketing* 43, (Fall 1979), pp. 103–11.

Yi, Y. "A Critical Review of Customer Satisfaction." In *Review of Marketing.* Ed. Valerie A. Zeithaml. Chicago: American Marketing Association, 1990, pp. 68–123.

CHAPTER 6

MARKET POTENTIAL
AND FORECASTING

OVERVIEW

To make intelligent decisions regarding which strategy to follow and what level of activity to plan for, managers must try to estimate the results (typically in terms of sales in units) of various actions. This requires knowing what might happen (potential) and what we think will happen (forecast). This chapter addresses developing potential estimates and forecasts. Since potentials are often an input to a forecast, we discuss these first.

Definitions

The terms *potential, forecast,* and *quota* are used in many contexts. For this book, we adopt the following definitions:

Potential: The maximum reasonably attainable under a given set of conditions (or, in older English, what "thou might achieve"). Put differently, sales achieved through 100 percent distribution and heavy advertising and promotion.

Forecast: What you expect to achieve under a given set of conditions (what "thou should achieve").

Quota: What you are expected to achieve (what "thou best achieve").

These definitions suggest several points:

First, potentials and forecasts exist at both the industry/market and firm level.

	Expectations	Possibilities
Firm	Sales forecast	Sales potential
Industry	Market forecast	Market potential

Since our focus is on firm-level planning, we will concentrate on the sales forecast and discuss market forecasts and market potentials as means to reach the sales forecast.

Second, both potentials and forecasts depend on a set of conditions. These conditions can be divided into four major categories of what customers do, what the firm does, what competitors do, and what occurs in the general environment (economy, culture).

Third, potentials and forecasts are time dependent. What may not be possible in the short run may be attainable in the longer term. While strategic plans depend on long-term potentials, annual plans focus primarily on short-run potentials and forecasts. But beware. By optimizing short-run decisions, the firm may make what in the long run is a less than optimal series of decisions. That is why products are often assigned different objectives, such as increasing sales (when the long-term potential seems large and increasing) or maximizing cash flow (when the long-term potential appears low).

Fourth, quotas are essentially required levels of performance. While these ideally should be flexible as conditions warrant, they are typically treated as "nonnegotiable" demands.

Why They Are Used

The major uses of potential estimates are essentially threefold:

1. To Make Entry/Exit Decisions. Potentials (both market and sales) are key numbers in the strategic decisions about what markets to be in.

2. To Make Location Decisions. Manufacturing plants, distribution facilities, and retail stores tend to be located based on potential estimates.

3. As an Input to Forecasts. The major use of potentials in annual planning is as a basis for the sales forecast. This suggests a forecast can be viewed as the product of potential times the percent of potential expected to be achieved.

The major uses of forecasts are:

1. To Answer "What If" Questions. In considering which strategy and tactics to follow, the key information is an estimate of the outcomes of the various strategies and tactics, typically the sales and profit levels. The simplest "what if" question is what will happen next year if everything remains as it has been in the past, which makes the forecast basically an extrapolation.

2. To Set Budgets.   Sales forecasts become the basis of a budget since they specify both sales levels to be attained and, by implication, the resources needed. All pro forma income statements use a sales forecast as their basis.

3. To Establish a Basis for a Monitoring System.   Deviations from forecasts warn managers to reexamine a market and their strategy. For example, assume we had market potential estimates and sales data for several regions (Figure 6–1). In this case, the relation between potential and

FIGURE 6–1

Hypothetical Sales versus Market Potential Data

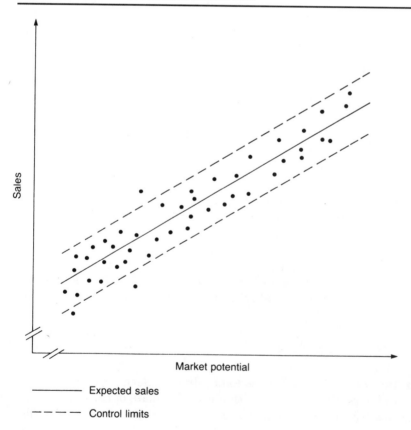

actual sales is quite close. Therefore, the sales-versus-potential curve could be used for evaluating performance. Those regions where sales fall above the upper control limit would be classified as "good," while those where sales fall below the lower control limit would be "bad." While these results could then be tied directly to compensation for regional managers, this might not be appropriate. For example, a region that did very well could have done so because an important competitor folded or a major promotion was staged. Similarly, a region that did badly could have done so because of at least five reasons:

- Increased competitive pressure.
- Overestimated potential.
- Nonoptimal strategy determination and/or execution.
- Capacity limitations.
- Inadequate effort by the industry as a whole.

Consequently, the best use of forecasts (or market potential estimates) for control is as a warning device to indicate when a region is doing especially well or poorly. One should then attempt to determine why (good management, competition, luck, and so on) the region had an exceptional performance and learn something from it.

By contrast, quotas are used to establish goals. When there are sales goals, for example, they indicate to regional managers and salespeople what they are expected to achieve. Also, sales goals establish standards for performance evaluation, typically at a very disaggregated (e.g., salesperson) level.

What Must Be Forecast

This chapter focuses on the sales forecast. Thus, potentials serve mainly as an input to forecasts, and quotas are essentially an apportioning of the forecast to various subunits of the organization. Sales forecasts then become the basis for pro forma income (profit and loss) statements, which become the summary of the impact of the budget in the plan as well as the basis for selecting among several strategies.

As mentioned earlier, a good forecast takes into account four major categories of variables: customer behavior, company actions, competitive actions, and the environment. Company actions are assumed to be predictable; although in companies not organized around a product management concept, many decisions, such as advertising and pricing, may be made in a piecemeal rather than an integrated fashion. By contrast, customer and competitive actions are hard to forecast and come out of the customer and competitive analysis parts of the plan. The general environment consists of such elements as state of the economy and key industries, demographic changes in the population, and costs of basic resources. While these elements can be forecast by the company, they are generally derived from secondary sources, such as government projections, and appear in the industry analysis and/or the planning assumptions section of the plan. Environmental changes affect the plan mainly through their impact on customer and competitive behavior, and they are so crucial that they are treated separately here.

The forecasting phase of the planning process ideally can be thought of as the process of assessing the possible outcome under all reasonably likely combinations of the four basic determinants of outcome. Notice, however, this suggests that achieving forecasts by varying only company decisions without considering competitive reactions is, unless the competitors are asleep, insufficient. The forecasting process can be viewed as a process of filling out a three-dimensional grid (Figure 6–2) with the likely outcomes.

It is useful to emphasize that the forecast in each cell should not be a single number but a range of possible outcomes. Thus, while a forecast of 21,274.43 parts may sound better than 21,000 ± 4,000, it may be misleading and an example of foolish precision. Put differently, do not expect forecasts to six decimal places, especially when such precision is not crucial to making a sound decision.

While a "best-guess" forecast is useful, so is data on the upper and lower bounds of the outcome. Knowing the range of likely results is crucial for strategy selection. A firm may be unwilling to undertake a strategy with a high expected result (e.g., a profit of $8 million) that also has a reasonably likely disastrous result (e.g., loss of $5 million). Conversely, a firm may be willing to gamble on a possible large return (e.g., a profit of $20 million) even if the likely result is a small profit or even a loss. It is also useful to know the likely range of outcomes for purposes of monitoring and

FIGURE 6–2
Format for Forecasts

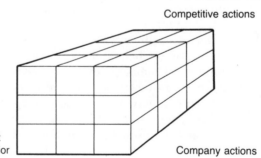

Competitive actions

General environment
and customer behavior

Company actions

control. For example, a drop of 30 percent below the forecast may be within the expected range and therefore not necessarily cause for a major reanalysis in one situation, whereas in a different situation a 15 percent drop below the forecast may signal a serious problem.

Producing a forecast for each possible situation is a tedious task at best. Consequently, it is desirable to limit the task to, say, three environments (expected, benign, and hostile) and a limited number of competitive postures (e.g., status quo, more aggressive). This limitation, however, should be made with two points in mind. First, the initial forecasts may suggest a promising avenue or potential disaster that may lead to refining the scenarios. Second, the assumptions made here are crucial; therefore, it is desirable to designate them formally as "planning assumptions."

Level of Accuracy Needed

Obviously, more accuracy in a forecast is better than less. Also, assuming a reasonably intelligent forecasting procedure is being employed (something one should *not* generally assume), then the only way to get a better forecast is to spend more time, effort, and money. Since increasing forecast accuracy has diminishing marginal returns (to make the range of a forecast half as large will generally at least quadruple the cost of a forecast), at some point the cost of improving the forecast will exceed the benefit.

The benefit of a better forecast usually is greater when (*a*) the price of the product being forecast is high in either absolute or relative terms ($10,000 may not be much to IBM but it is to me); (*b*) the product demand is relatively volatile; and (*c*) the cost of an error in forecasting (including reorder cost and the cost of being out of stock—which may include the long-term loss of a disenchanted customer) is high. The cost of a better forecast increases as (*a*) the number of items or product forms increases (e.g., machine tool A with feature X, with features X and Z, and so on); (*b*) the forecasting method becomes more complicated to use; and (*c*) the forecast (and its basis) is difficult to communicate to others in the organization. (Generally, review committees prefer not to hear about Fourier series, correlated errors, and so on.)

This chapter proceeds as follows. First, we discuss methods for forecasting market potential. A more detailed discussion of forecasting methods follows, with the use of regression analysis emphasized. The chapter then presents an example and discusses such issues as presentation of forecasts and gaining agreement about a forecast. The chapter closes with a summary of key points. (While it might be interesting to omit a summary to assess the reaction, it would be incompatible with expectations and hence decrease the potential for the book. We decided it wouldn't be *that* interesting.)

ESTIMATING MARKET AND SALES POTENTIAL: BASICS

Market potential may be estimated in a variety of ways, and the details involved depend on the particular industry and product under consideration. This section suggests some general approaches to assessing potential.

Clearly, past sales data are useful to have, and provide both a potential estimate and a sales forecast for a stable market. In new markets, however, such data may be unavailable, inaccurate, or unduly influenced by isolated events. Also, just because such data are available does *not* mean other data should be ignored.

Figure 6–3 summarizes a general process for deriving potential estimates (which is useful for forecast development as well). Notice the feedback from estimate to judgment, which then may alter the forecast. It is both reasonable and potentially dangerous to revise forecasts when the results are "no good"; this process can lead to either better models or a search for the model that gives the "right" answer.

The exact data collected and calculations used depend on the type of situation encountered. Nonetheless, some general categories of data exist.

Secondary Sources

Before spending too much time developing one's own potential estimates, it is advisable to consult available sources.

- *Government sources.* Market size estimates are available for many industries from sources such as the U.S. Department of Commerce and

FIGURE 6–3
Deriving Potential Estimates

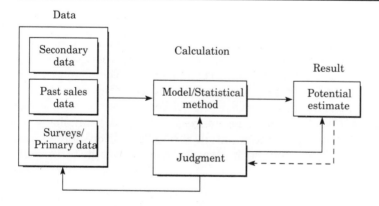

the Bureau of the Census (e.g., *Survey of Current Business, Current Industrial Reports*). Even when specific forecasts for the industry or product are not available, government data may be useful as input to the potential estimate. Examples include breakdowns of industry by location, size, and Standard Industrial Classification (SIC) code and forecasts of general economic conditions.

- *Trade associations.*
- *Private companies.* A number of private companies track and forecast sales for various industries (e.g., Find/SVP, Predicasts, Morton). Some also survey capital spending plans (e.g., McGraw-Hill) and consumer sentiment and plans (e.g., Survey Research Center at the University of Michigan).
- *Financial analysts.* Industry specialists often provide forecasts and/ or potential estimates for various industries (e.g., Gartner Group for computers). Some of this material finds its way into the popular press (e.g., *Fortune, Forbes, Business Week*).

While many sources of forecasts exist, the competency and accuracy may not be high. (While it is comforting to assume that published forecasts are accurate and done by experts, both the accuracy and expertise are often suspect. Think of it this way: The person who prepared the forecast may have been a classmate of yours!) To understand/assess the value of a forecast (whether provided by an outsider or a subordinate), at least a rudimentary knowledge of how forecasts are constructed is required. This chapter therefore goes into some detail on forecasting methods in the hope that the reader will become a more intelligent consumer of forecasts.

Primary Data/Surveys

Primary data-based potential numbers straddle the line between potentials and forecasts. Since, for example, surveys typically ask "What will you do?" or "If X occurs, what will you do?" they are mainly forecast oriented. So, rather than discuss the survey approach to establishing market potential in detail here, we defer that discussion to the section "Sales Forecasting Methods."

Assessing the Value of a New or Growing Product: Initial Purchase

In considering both the saturation level (ultimate potential) and the time pattern of development, it is useful to consider the product vis-à-vis its major (and presumably older) competitor. This can be accomplished by considering the three major dimensions of relative advantage, risk, and compatibility.

Relative Advantage

In terms of benefits provided, is the new product superior in all respects and by what amount? Noticeably superior benefits will increase both the saturation level and the rate at which the level is achieved. Also, in general, relative advantage of the new product will increase over time as various modifications and line extensions appear.

Risk

The greater the risk involved (financial, possible impact on product quality if a new component fails, and so on), the lower the probability that someone will buy the new product. Typically, risk—at least in terms of price—tends to drop over time, thus increasing the saturation level.

Compatibility

The fewer and less major the changes required to adopt a new product, the faster it will be adopted. Compatibility issues relate not only to the customers but also to middlemen, the company itself (e.g., sales staff), and, if the customer uses a certain product as a component in a product, their customer as well. Therefore, if a chemical company is planning to manufacture a new product, issues of manufacturing compatibility and sales staff effort arise within the company along with the behavior of wholesalers (assuming the product is sold through that channel), customer problems (Is retooling required?), and eventual customer acceptance (e.g., it took a long time to convince customers that plastic parts were acceptable in automobiles, even when both molders and the auto manufacturers were convinced). Again, as in the case of risk, incompatibility tends to decrease over time. Finally, incompatibility may be primarily psychological (i.e., "We just don't do things that way here"), and failure to consider the psychological barriers to adoption is often disastrous, at least in assessing short-term potential.

Role of Analogous Products

Examining the pattern of use and adoption of analogous products or services is often useful, especially for growing or new products. For either a new or growing product, the adoption pattern of previous products of a similar type provides a clue to both the likely pattern and rate of adoption and the eventual saturation level.

The problem with using analogies is that two products are rarely perfectly comparable. For them to be reasonably comparable, both the newer product and its older analog should be targeted to a similar market; be similar in perceived value, both in toto and in terms of the major benefits provided (e.g., convenience); and be similar in price. Under these criteria, a microwave oven could be compared to a dishwasher (both are targeted at households, stress convenience/time saving, and cost in the hundreds of dollars). By contrast, a mainframe computer (circa 1960) and a microcomputer (circa 1990) are not analogous, even though one is a direct descendant of the other, since the target market (a company versus individuals), value perceived (number crunching and billing versus convenience and word processing), and price (a million versus a few hundred dollars) are all dramatically different. Similarly, a home trash compactor and a dishwasher differed substantially on perceived value added and, therefore, a priori, one should have expected a much lower saturation level for trash compactors than for dishwashers.

Mature Product Potentials

The more mature a product, the more sales will come from past customers reordering the product. This reordering will come in two types. For a consumable product, the ordering of the product will be in proportion to the market need for the product (if an industrial product) or usage rate (if a consumer product). For a durable, ordering the product will often be to replace a worn-out product, to upgrade to get new features, or to add an additional model (e.g., a second color TV; see Bayus, Hong, and Labe, 1989).

ESTIMATING MARKET AND SALES POTENTIAL: METHODS

Judgment plays a crucial and ubiquitous role in the derivation of potential elements. It influences the type of data examined, the model used to derive the estimate, and often the estimate itself. While statistical knowledge is useful, logic or common sense is much more important. Therefore, the following methods are best viewed as aids to, rather than as substitutes for, judgment.

Pattern Extrapolation

For products where actual sales data are available, a common method of estimating potential is to use past data to project into the future. This can be done either by a simple examination of a graph of sales versus time or by some mathematical model based on the first few sales periods (see the section on "Sales Forecasting Methods" for examples). A serious problem with this procedure is that both the eventual level and the rate at which it is achieved depend on elements other than the physical product. For example, the potential for computers is clearly greater when the price is $3,000 rather than $3 million (Figure 6–4). Similarly, sales will tend to approach their ultimate level faster when more effort is put into selling the product (e.g., advertising or trade allowances). Also, the state of the economy affects the sales of most goods and services. Thus, pattern extrapolation can be misleading if any of the elements of the marketing mix or the general environment change. Since production experience tends to decrease the cost and, therefore, the price of most goods, and high technology goods in particular, this suggests a more thorough analysis is needed even when actual data are available.

The most useful form of actual data is sales in regions geographically separated from the region under consideration. Projections of potential in

FIGURE 6–4
Relation of Sales to the Marketing Mix

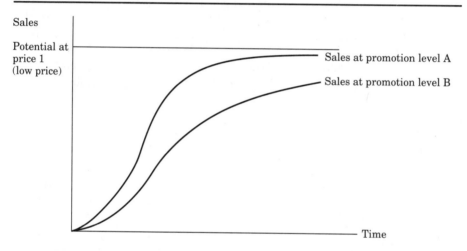

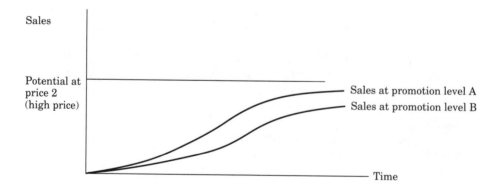

a new region can be made based on such variables as population in the target age group (for products such as foods) or number of businesses of a certain type (for products such as payroll services). Even when such regional information is available, however, the potential may differ widely for a variety of institutional and cultural reasons (e.g., the share of certain types of sterling silver flatware patterns varies widely among such areas as California, the South, and New England).

Analysis Based

In order to deduce the potential for a product, a basic approach is to first ascertain/estimate four things:

1. The type of people and/or organizations who might eventually buy the product category. This generally requires a careful analysis of the potential uses of the product and the relative value this product category has versus others in the various use situations.
2. The number of people and/or organizations of each type identified by step 1. Generally, this is based on secondary data such as population statistics or Department of Commerce data on businesses based on SIC codes.
3. The share of that type of people or business who will buy the product.
4. The rate at which buyers will consume the product (for a durable, this may be once).

Potential is then simply the product of 2, 3, and 4.

This four-step process is useful for getting an initial notion of a product's total potential. But estimating the fraction who will buy in a broadly defined segment of the population and the rate at which they will consume is often very difficult. Consider, for example, two products: a new copying system (an example of an industrial good) and a "diet" bourbon (a summer drink for the calorie conscious designed to compete with lighter alcoholic beverages such as vodka and wine coolers). Using the aggregate-level analysis just described, we would estimate potential as follows:

New copying system potential: (Number of businesses) × (Percent who have copiers) × (Fraction who "need" our new feature) × (Share who will buy new system) × (Number bought per firm).

Diet bourbon potential: (Population over 21) × (Percent who drink bourbon) × (Percent who are diet conscious) × (Fraction who will buy diet bourbon) × (Purchase rate).

While both these examples are logical applications of the "successive ratio" approach suggested above (also called the chain ratio method), there is tremendous uncertainty in terms of defining "number of businesses" and "percent who are diet conscious," much less what share will buy the innovation. For that reason, a segment-based approach as shown in Figure 6–5 is often useful for both predictive and diagnostic reasons.

Area Potential

Area potential is often derived by breaking down total sales by area. When sales data are available for a variety of regions along with some data on the characteristics of the regions, it is common to use an index that is a weighted combination of these characteristics to indicate the relative potential in the area. Many consumer goods companies use the *Sales & Marketing Management* Buying Power Index, which is: 0.2 (Population) + 0.3 (Retail sales) + 0.5 (Disposable income). This index is computed annually for various market areas of the United States. When population, retail sales, and disposable income are input as percent of the total United States, this index projects the percent of the product sold in the various regions. For established products, these weights may be estimated from the actual sales data by, for example, running a regression of sales versus various factors (e.g., number of schools in region). Product-related data such as sales of analogous products (here Xerox copiers) might also be used. In fact, sales of truly analogous products are often the best indicators of potential. An index approach for the hypothetical new copying system might be as follows:

Bases: Percent population in region (P)
Percent schools in region (S)
Percent retail businesses in region (RB)
Percent banks in region (B)
Percent offices in region (O)
Percent warehouses in region (WH)
Percent manufacturing facilities in region (MF)
Percent other businesses in region (OB)
Percent Xerox sales in region (XS)
Percent other copier sales in region (CS)

$$\text{Index} = W_1P + W_2S + W_3RB + W_4B + W_5O + W_6WH + W_7MF + W_8OB + W_9XS + W_{10}CS$$

A classic example of estimating area potential is provided by Hummel (1961) and described in Cox (1979). Hummel was concerned with estimating potential for a line of industrial truck casters manufactured by Bassick.

FIGURE 6–5
Diet Bourbon Potential

Segment	(1) Number	(2) Bourbon Consumption per Capita	(3) Percent Diet Conscious	(4) Consumption Rate	Segment Potential (1)×(2)×(3)×(4)
Single males 18–29					
Single females 18–29					
Married males 18–29					
Married females 18–29					
Single 30–55					
Married 30–55					
All 56 and older					
Total potential					

FIGURE 6–5 (concluded)
Copying System Potential

	(1)	(2)	(3)	(4)	
			Percent		*Segment*
		Percent	*Who Can*	*Number of*	*Potential*
		Who Use	*Use the New*	*Machines*	
	Number	*Copiers*	*Machines*	*Per User*	$(1) \times (2) \times (3) \times (4)$
Segment:					
Schools					
Retail businesses					
Banks					
Offices					
Warehouses					
Manufacturing facilities					
Other					
Total potential					

Segment

Using trade association data (American Supply and Machinery Manufacturers Association) for class V products (power transmission equipment, industrial rubber goods, materials handling equipment), he found a close association between class V shipments and sales. Based on this, area potentials were estimated, and strong and weak market areas were identified.

Another example is related to sales of printing ink. Sales were estimated for each user group based on the ratio of ink sales to total materials and supplies (Figure 6–6). For example, periodicals spent 3.5 percent of their material and supply budget on ink. Hence, the estimated San Francisco-Oakland SMSA printing ink sales would be $7,600,000 \times 0.035 = $266,000.

One final example of market potential estimation deals with the potential cargo volume for trucks between Atlanta and Los Angeles. One potential source of business would be beverages (SIC code 208). From the 1972 Census of Transportation, the amount shipped from California to the Southeast region was 87,000 tons. Assuming we are estimating potential for 1975, this must be updated. The Census of Manufacturers indicates a 35.8 percent increase in dollar sales. Deflating by the cost-of-living increase of 23.2 percent, this suggests 1975 tons $= (87,000) (1.358)(1/1.232) =$ 95,900. (Notice we have rounded off rather than to imply great precision.) Now it is necessary to convert general region-to-region shipment data into SMSA-to-SMSA shipment data. This could be done several ways, including using the census of manufacturing data on value-added and taking the ratio of Los Angeles SMSA to California and the Atlanta SMSA to the Southeast. The resulting market potential might then be: (95,900 tons) (Source ratio) (Destination ratio) = 9,050 tons.

In summary, market potential should be estimated systematically. Moreover, different approaches are needed for different situations (Figure 6–7). Blind adherence to a particular system, however, will often result in a poor estimate. (The original projection showed a worldwide demand for mainframe computers of 15 to 20 and the demand for Xerox copiers under 2,000.) In short, both push numbers and think.

SALES FORECASTING METHODS

Conceptually, a sales forecast can be seen as an extension of the market potential estimate. For a new product, this can be derived as follows:

$$
\begin{array}{c}
\text{Sales} \\
\text{forecast}
\end{array}
=
\begin{array}{c}
\text{Market} \\
\text{potential}
\end{array}
\times
\begin{array}{c}
\text{Percent of potential} \\
\text{attained by} \\
\text{product category}
\end{array}
\times
\begin{array}{c}
\text{"Our" share} \\
\text{of product} \\
\text{category}
\end{array}
$$

For existing products, this procedure is useful conceptually. For predictive purposes, however, it is more common to use actual sales data as the basis

FIGURE 6–6

Market Potential for Printing Ink in the San Francisco–Oakland SMSA

Industry	SIC Code	Materials Consumed, United States			San Francisco–Oakland SMSA	
		All Materials and Supplies (millions)	Printing Inks (millions)	Proportion of Printing Inks to all Materials and Supplies	All Materials and Supplies (millions)	Market Potential ($)
Newspapers	2711	$1,438.2	$ 25.6	.018	$35.9	$ 646,200
Periodicals	2721	510.3	18.2	.035	7.6	266,000
Book publishing	2731	252.4	3.5	.014	3.8	53,200
Book printing	2732	224.4	11.5	.051	2.6	132,600
Commercial printing	275	2,112.3	139.3	.066	67.0	4,422,000
Manifold business forms	2761	348.9	4.4	.013	13.0	169,000
Total						$5,689,000

Note: Data on materials consumed, United States, drawn from *1967 Census of Manufacturers—Vol. 1, Summary and Subject Statistics*; data on materials consumed in San Francisco–Oakland SMSA drawn from Vol. III, Part 1 of same *Census—Area Statistics*.

Source: Adapted with permission of Macmillan Publishing Company from *Marketing Research* by Donald S. Tull and Del I. Hawkins, p. 581. Copyright © 1976 by Macmillan Publishing Company.

FIGURE 6–7

Suggested Approach to Estimating Potential for Different Situations

Situation	Key Data	Calculation Method
Relatively mature product	Past sales Judgment: is a critical change imminent?	Extrapolation
Growing product	Past sales Judgment: is a major competitive change imminent?	Extrapolation using a saturation level
New industrial good	Secondary: economic conditions Judgment: target segments (e.g., SIC codes)	Segment buildup
New consumer good: durable	Secondary: market segments (e.g., demographic) Survey plus judgment: rate of adoption	Segment buildup
New consumer good: frequently purchased	Secondary: market segments (demographic) Primary: trial and repeat rate	New product forecasting model

for the forecast. The remainder of this section, therefore, describes common methods for projecting sales and their pros and cons. There are three basic types of forecasting: qualitative, extrapolative (qualitative and quantitative), and model building. This section outlines some of the major alternatives of these three types. We devote particular attention to regression-based forecasting since it is widely used, something many readers may have at least heard of, and very versatile.

Qualitative

Judgment

The least complicated forecasting method is the use of expert judgment (guessing might be a more appropriate description). We simply ask someone what the future will be and record the answer. If the expert chosen happens to know the Delphic Oracle or to be a mystic, the forecast can be excellent. Unfortunately, it is hard to know whether someone can predict the future a priori. The key to the value of expert judgment is the ability of the expert to recall from memory relevant data and assimilate the data in making a guess. While judgment is often unsystematic, it can be useful and can overcome some of the limitations of quantitative techniques. Probably the best use of judgment, however, is to adjust the results of quantitative procedures rather than as the sole forecasting tool. Alternatively, judgment-based decision trees similar to those described in Chapter 2 can be used in developing forecasts.

Polling of Experts

The polling-of-experts method is really an extension of expert judgment under a safety-in-numbers assumption. Rather than trust a single expert, this approach collects forecasts from a number of experts. The forecasts are then combined in a particular manner, such as a simple or weighted average. (Since some experts are presumably more expert than others, their forecasts are weighted more heavily.) This method thus produces a forecast that is "neutral" and will (like most methods) avoid the unusual or radically different result. In fact, the most useful information from polling experts may be the range of the forecasts and the reasons given to support the forecasts rather than their average.

Panel Consensus

The panel consensus method of forecasting consists of putting a group of experts in a room and waiting for them to agree on a forecast. Aside from problems with dominant group members, this method generally produces (assuming the panel members eventually agree) the conventional wisdom. Since experts sometimes are wrong (e.g., remember the new math, stock market forecasts, and the impossibility of an international oil cartel?), the experts' opinions can be deceptively impressive.

A variety of "fancy" techniques are available for gaining panel consensus. One of the best known of these is the Delphi procedure, which is often used to set budgets. The process begins by asking a number of individuals to produce a forecast. An outside person then collects the forecasts and calculates the average. Next, the outside person gives to each participant both the original forecast and the average. At this point, each participant is asked to reconsider his or her initial forecast. Typically (and hopefully), the participants then change their forecasts to more nearly conform to the average. If the process is repeated several times, generally consensus is achieved.

Survey Based

In estimating the demand for a product, one approach is to survey potential customers, who are after all "experts." While obvious, this approach is not without perils. For example, the usual issues of nonresponse bias and inaccurate responses arise. Moreover, two questions are especially troublesome: whom to survey and how to deal with the results.

Whom to Survey?   When conducting surveys for industrial products, it is not at all clear whom to talk to within a company even if one knows which company to talk to. For example, when the Federal Communications Commission (FCC) invited bids for cellular mobile phone licenses in various cities, it required a study of market potential as part of the application. Most companies attempted to address this by phone surveys contacting the manager of telecommunications (or someone having a similar title) and asking about how many phones the company would use. However, these managers might not have known how many were needed or had much authority over such acquisitions.

Regarding which companies to survey first requires specifying the potential segments and then ensuring there are enough of each type included to get a reasonable estimate. Unfortunately, if there are 10 target groups and five size variations per group, this leads to a large sample size.

Figure 6–8 shows the number of firms by employee number in several SIC codes. How would you apportion the sample and still be able to represent each segment "accurately"? The answer requires a balance between a stratified sample based on assumed variability of demand and getting a reasonable number in each cell.

How to Deal with the Results?   Considering again the example in Figure 6–8, it would be preferable if the results made sense, but sometimes they are inconsistent. For example, assume the average firm sales for the five size categories in Figure 6–8 were as follows: 192, 181, 490, 360, and 2,000.

Do you treat them as "truth," or do you smooth them so bigger firms spend more? Moreover, what do you do if total demand comes out three times what was expected? Do you scale every estimate down by one third?

In summary, then, while surveys may produce a useful number, they are equally likely to produce numbers that, without "creative" manipulation, appear on the surface to be wrong.

Extrapolation: Qualitative

As a starting point for an alternative to expert judgment, a variety of extrapolation procedures exist. Two of these are essentially qualitative/judgmental in nature—last period + X percent and graphical eyeball.

Last Period + X Percent
One of the most common approaches to forecasting is to estimate the percent change expected in the variable to be forecast. This is especially common in deriving annual sales forecasts for major product breakdowns. For

FIGURE 6–8
Potential Customers by Industry and Size

SIC	Industry	Percent of 1981 Demand Accounted for	Total Number of Firms	Number of Employees				
				50–99	100–249	250–499	500–999	1,000 or More
28	Chemical	20	7,012	754	610	293	193	123
29	Petroleum	20	444	57	73	53	42	22
33	Primary metals	10	1,889	266	352	181	74	108
12	Bituminous	2	4,050	295	272	166	80	11
20	Food	5	10,032	1,114	957	393	153	57
22	Textile	2	1,786	207	229	187	160	50
26	Paper and allied products	10	1,314	184	235	116	104	58
34	Fabricated metal	3	4,568	310	111	16	2	—
36	Electrical equipment	3	942	90	109	94	43	35
49	Electricity, gas	25	5,250	766	588	214	97	69
	Total		37,287	4,043	3,536	1,713	948	533

Expected Maximum Spending by Size Category

Employee Size	Maximum Spending
50 to 99	$ 100,000
100 to 249	200,000
250 to 499	500,000
500 to 999	750,000
1,000 or more	1,000,000

example, we may forecast dishwasher sales in dollars as last year's plus 6 percent.

Graphical Eyeball

Similar to the last period + X percent method, the graphical eyeball approach requires plotting past data. Then the next value is "eyeballed" to match the past pattern (Figure 6–9). This method does by graph what many quantitative techniques do by number crunching.

Extrapolation: Quantitative

A variety of quantitative extrapolation procedures are also available. Some of the most commonly used are given below. For a more complete discussion, see Wheelwright and Makridakis (1985).

Moving Average

Moving averages, an old forecasting standby, are widely used to reduce the noise in data to uncover the underlying pattern. In doing so, it is important to recognize that past data have at least four major components:

1. Base value.
2. Trend.
3. Cycle(s) (seasonality).
4. Random.

Moving averages essentially smooth out random variation to make the patterns (trends and cycles) more apparent.

FIGURE 6–9
Geographical Eyeball Forecasting

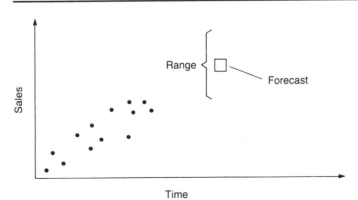

Complex moving-average models are available for estimating trends and cycles. For purposes of introduction, however, we will consider only the simple moving-average approach. A three-period moving average of sales at time t is given by

$$\hat{S}_t = \frac{S_{t-1} + S_t + S_{t+1}}{3}$$

This equation implies that (a) each data point used is weighted equally and (b) no trend or cycle is accounted for. To see how this method works, consider the three-month moving average for the eight periods of data in Figure 6–10. As can be readily seen, the fluctuation in values is much less in moving averages than in the raw data, and a consistent trend of increase of about 10 units per period becomes apparent. Forecasts would now be based on the pattern of moving averages rather than on the raw data.

Moving-average methods can be extended to track trends and seasonal patterns as well. For example, to smooth a trend, simply calculate the period-to-period changes and average them as in Figure 6–10. However, regression analysis (to be discussed later) has generally replaced moving averages as a forecasting tool for all but the simplest situations.

Exponential Smoothing

A second approach to extrapolation is exponential smoothing. As in the case of moving averages, this approach smooths out the random variation in period-to-period values. Trends and cycles are estimated (smoothed) separately. Like moving averages, this approach has been largely replaced by time series regression.

Time Series Regression

A third way to extrapolate data is by using regression analysis with time (period) as the independent variable. Time series regression produces

FIGURE 6–10

Hypothetical Sales Example

Period	Sales	Three-Period Moving Average	Trend	Three-Period Trend Average
1	100	—	—	—
2	110	105	+10	—
3	105	115	−5	+10
4	130	125	+25	−10
5	140	130	+10	+5
6	120	140	−20	+10
7	160	152	+40	+11.33
8	175	—	+15	—

estimates of the base level (intercept) and trend (slope). Seasonal patterns can be handled outside the regression (i.e., by removing the estimated seasonal component from the values of the dependent variable before performing the regression) or by various "tricks" within the regression (e.g., using dummy variables; see Wildt, 1977). Ignoring seasonality, the model is simply

$$\text{Sales} = a + b(\text{Time})$$

Addressing the same eight-period example in this manner produces the result in Figure 6–11. The forecast for period 10 based on this model would thus be

$$\hat{S}_{10} = 85.4 + 9.88(10) = 184.2$$

In addition to the basic forecast, regression produces several bonuses, including:

Measure of Goodness of Fit. R^2 is the percent of sales variance that was explained by the predictor variables (in this case, a time trend). A bigger R^2 generally indicates better predictive ability.

Standard Error of Estimate. $S_{Y.X}$ quantifies the range of likely outcomes. Typically, a prediction is given by $\hat{S} \pm KS_{Y.X}$. (For most situations, $K = 2$ will prove adequate.)

Actually, all three methods, moving average, exponential smoothing, and time series regression, are similar. They differ in which past results they use to develop their estimates. Moving averages weight some of the

FIGURE 6–11
Time Series Regression Example

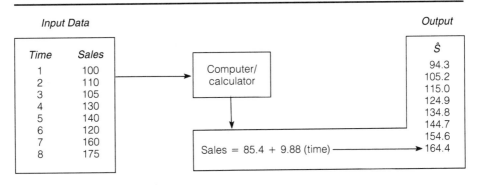

Input Data			Output
			$\hat{S}$
Time	*Sales*		94.3
1	100	Computer/calculator	105.2
2	110		115.0
3	105		124.9
4	130		134.8
5	140		144.7
6	120		154.6
7	160	Sales = 85.4 + 9.88 (time)	164.4
8	175		

most recent data points equally. Exponential smoothing weights all the data points unequally with the most recent having the most weight, the next most recent the next highest weight, and so forth. Finally, regression typically weights all the points equally, although unequal weights can be used. Choosing among the three is therefore a matter of taste, availability, and experience. Given our familiarity with regression, we use regression when the choice arises. More advanced forms of time series analysis such as Box-Jenkins methods are beyond the scope of this book. (See Appendix 6A for a somewhat more complete discussion of time series regression.)

Epidemic Models

One approach to forecasting sales of a new product assumes that initial sales of the product will follow the same shape curve (Figure 6–12) as an epidemic (which, given some new products, may be an apt analogy). This curve implies there will be a slow start during which the innovators become "infected," followed by a growth period in which sales of the product (or the disease) spread rapidly through the population. Sales then slow as the number of eventual buyers (people susceptible to the disease) is approached. Such a model has been presented by Bass (1969) and used at companies such as Eastman Kodak to forecast sales of new consumer durables in terms of when they would peak and how big the peak would be. While such models may be imperfect predictors, the basic notion of a pattern of sales growth and the existence of a saturation level are useful in considering any

FIGURE 6–12
Trial over Time for a New Product

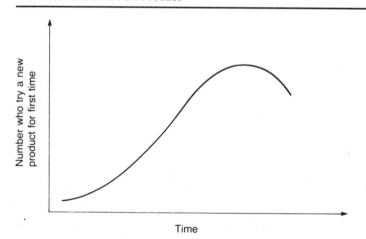

Time

type of forecast. (See Appendix 6B for a more detailed discussion of epidemic models.)

Regression Models

Regression models are the most widely used form of models in marketing research. These models are developed in three stages. First, the variables that are assumed to affect the dependent variable are specified as:

$$\text{Sales} = f(\text{our price, competitors' prices, our advertising,}$$
$$\text{competitors' advertising, disposable income})$$

Next, a model that indicates the form of the relation between the independent variables and sales is specified. These models are generally linear, such as:

$$
\begin{aligned}
\text{Sales in cartons } (S) = {}& \text{Constant} \\
& + B_1 \text{ (our price)} \\
& + B_2 \text{ (our advertising)} \\
& + B_3 (\text{disposable income})
\end{aligned}
$$

The model is then estimated by means of regression analysis:

$$
\begin{aligned}
S = {}& 1.2 - .2 \text{ (Price in dollars)} + 1.3 \text{ (Advertising in dollars)} \\
& + .1 \text{ (Disposable income in \$ billions)}
\end{aligned}
$$

Regression models serve two basic uses—sales forecasting and answering "what if" questions.

Sales Forecasting
To use regression models to forecast, one must first forecast the values of the independent variables. If this is difficult, then regression becomes less useful as a straight forecasting device. Put differently, in building a multiple-regression model for forecasting, make sure the independent variables are easily forecast. Also, every forecast should have a range. Typically, a range of about two standard errors of estimate is used.

Answering "What If" Questions
In our example,

$$B_1 = \text{Marginal effect of changing our price}$$
$$B_2 = \text{Marginal effect of changing our advertising share}$$

If you make the rather large assumption that the relation between price and sales is causal rather than just correlational, you can answer a question such as "What if I increase advertising by \$10?" In this case, a \$10 increase in advertising would lead to a $(1.3)(10) = 13$ carton change in sales.

Another type of regression model assumes sales in the next period depend on sales in the previous period plus other variables (e.g., GNP, advertising, price). These blend time series and contemporaneous effects in a single model. These models, which include the "carryover" effect of repeat sales, often provide good fits for fairly mature products. Their main advantage, however, is in estimating the effect of advertising, price, and so forth on current sales, rather than as "just" forecasting models.

Developing the Model

Developing a regression model is typically a trial-and-error process. The first stage involves selecting variables to consider including and is usually based on a combination of data availability and plausibility (do the independent variables logically affect the dependent variable and are the forecasts reasonable?). In determining the type of variables to include, it is generally useful to consider what variables in each of the following categories might be most appropriate:

1. Customer status and traits (e.g., the size of the population in a particular age category).
2. "Our" marketing programs (e.g., advertising).
3. Competitive behavior (e.g., new product introductions).
4. General environment (e.g., gross national product).

Having generated data for a set of variables, the next step is to generate correlations among the variables. Examining these allows quick identification of those variables that are most highly correlated with sales. It also provides a quick indication of the degree of redundancy among the potential predictors. Dealing with redundancy (known to econometricians as multicollinearity) can involve relatively sophisticated (or at least complicated) procedures (e.g., factor analysis). However, a simple approach is to include in a regression model only one of a set of highly correlated variables. For example, if you use macroeconomic variables such as GNP, disposable income, personal income, and so on, you will find they are highly correlated. For most situations, it is best to pick just one of these variables to include in the model.

Next several different regression models are run and evaluated. The bases for the evaluation are typically:

1. *Goodness of Fit.* All other things equal, the model that fits the (past) data the best (has the largest R^2 and the lowest standard error of estimate) is preferred. Similarly, models that predict situations not

used to estimate/calibrate the model (a so-called holdout sample) better are preferred.

2. *Sensible Coefficients.* Having plausible signs (e.g., the impact of price on sales is normally negative) and magnitudes is important for one's own confidence in the results and crucial for explaining/selling the results to intelligent others.

3. *Significant Coefficients.* If a variable is not significant, it is often appropriate to *consider* dropping it from the model. However, since lack of significance can be due to redundancy or simply a small number of data points, wholesale pruning of insignificant variables is not recommended.

4. *Parsimony.* In general, simple models are better both to use and to explain to others. Also, there is often a severe limitation on data (e.g., only eight years' worth), which means a model with more than two or three predictor variables is generally very unstable.

5. *Ease of Application.* Both data availability (including the availability of reasonable forecasts for the predictor variables) and easy communicability are positive assets for a model.

Dealing with Outliers

Anyone dealing with forecasting soon discovers that most data sets contain a few observations that are very far from the forecast value. These tend to both distort the model and to decrease the fit of the model. A question that immediately arises is what to do with such outliers. Actually, two very different answers appear: spend some time attempting to explain the outliers or reduce their impact on the forecast by "neutralizing" them.

Studying Them. This approach is often the most useful since frequently the outliers contain substantial information. For example, if a sales versus potential regression were run with data on 79 territories, sales in some of the territories could be abnormally low or high. By examining the characteristics of the "outliers," one often discovers an explanation that leads to altering the model by adding one or more additional variables to it. Examination of outliers is often the most expedient way to consider model modification.

Neutralizing Them. Assuming either (*a*) no explanation can be found for outliers, suggesting they are simply unusual, random happenings; (*b*) an explanation can be found that is hopefully or genuinely a onetime occurrence (e.g., an earthquake); or (*c*) the forecast is not critical (e.g., a very minor product), then it may be more beneficial simply to remove the outliers. One other approach is to just ignore their impact. This will work if they are randomly distributed (Figure 6–13A). Unfortunately, a small number of grouped outliers, as in Figure 6–13B, can severely distort the forecast line and hence the forecasts. Therefore, it is often useful to reduce their impact on the forecast.

Reducing the impact is typically done by replacing the actual value with a value that is closer to the value one would expect based on the other observations. This data manipulation can range from the extreme of substituting the forecast for the actual to less severe "filtering" approaches that replace the actual data with, for example, the 95 percent confidence interval value for the observation. A more extreme approach is to simply disregard the observation. In addition to seeming "unfair," all these approaches run the risk of producing results (e.g., R^2s) that are falsely impressive and hence lead the user of the forecast to underestimate the uncertainty that exists.

FIGURE 6–13

A. Random outliers

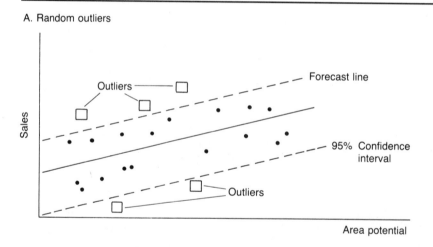

B. Grouped outliers

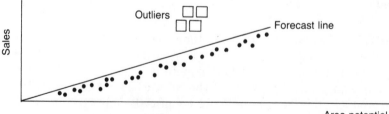

When the identity of the outlier is known and the cause deduced, it is possible to subjectively adjust the actual value by the impact of the cause. For example, one might assume a strike that lasted one of four weeks in a given period reduced sales by 25 percent; consequently, we would multiply actual sales by 1.33 to get actual sales as they would have been without the strike. (This assumes no carryover effects of sales across periods, which for all but the most perishable commodities—for example, fresh melon or newspapers—is a bad assumption.) While this approach is subjective, if the goal is to produce forecasts based on the underlying trend, then such manipulation may be the most appropriate way to produce believable forecasts.

Nonlinear Relations

Most regression forecasting models are linear. That is, they are of the form:

$$Y = B_0 + B_1 X_1 + B_2 X_2 + \ldots$$

where X_1 and X_2 are the predictor variables and Y represents sales.

In some cases, you may expect nonlinear relations. For example, you may believe there are diminishing returns to advertising. This can be handled in this framework by, for example, a logarithmic formulation:

$$Y = B_0 + B_1(\log \text{advertising})$$

One model that has been used fairly extensively is a multiplicative model:

$$Y = B_0 X_1^{B_1} X_2^{B}$$

which can be rewritten and estimated (but not perfectly efficiently) with a standard regression program:

$$\log Y = B_0^* + B_1(\log X_1) + B_2(\log X_2).$$

While nonlinear model forms are fairly unreliable for long-run forecasting, they sometimes are useful for one-period-ahead forecasts. However, most users tend to stick with linear models.

Making Forecasts

In order to make forecasts with a regression model, it is necessary to know or forecast the values of the predictor variables (e.g., advertising) in the next period. When these are known, a reasonable forecast includes a "best guess" obtained by substituting in the known values, a pessimistic forecast (typically the best guess minus two standard errors of estimate), and an optimistic forecast (the best guess plus two standard errors of estimate). Since, however, the predictor variables are rarely known with certainty, it is useful to construct both optimistic and pessimistic scenarios involving these variables and also generate forecasts based on these. The resulting three by three table (see Figure 6–14) gives a much clearer picture of the uncertainty inherent in the market (and what it depends on) than the best-guess forecast alone. While managers like to have *the* forecast, they *should* be given information like that in Figure 6–14. (Of course, that is easier for the authors, both of whom have tenure, to say than it is for a junior person facing a demanding boss.)

The impact of uncertainty about predictor variables can be shown more dramatically graphically (Figure 6–15). The true range is considerably larger than the range implied by using the standard error of the regression as a basis for estimating uncertainty. This means that unless you are fairly certain of what the value of the predictor variable will be, it doesn't help forecast very much. Hence, variables that are easy to predict (e.g., year, GNP) are, ceteris paribus, more useful as predictors than variables that are themselves unpredictable (e.g., consumer sentiment, commodity prices).

Simultaneous Equation Models

To improve the accuracy of a forecast for a particularly important variable (e.g., oil prices), it is often necessary to consider the interactions between this variable and other variables. For example, the price of oil influences the price of food, and the price of food influences the price of oil. To model such interdependency, systems of equations are specified. The parameters

FIGURE 6–14

Format Matrix for Reporting a Regression Model Based Forecast

	Forecast		
Scenario	Pessimistic Forecast − $2S_{Y.X}$	Best-Guess Forecast	Optimistic Forecast + $2S_{Y.X}$
Pessimistic: No change in GNP Advertising down 10 percent			
Best guess: GNP up 3 percent Advertising up 10 percent			
Optimistic: GNP up 5 percent Advertising up 25 percent			

of these models are then estimated by simultaneous equation regression. Using these models requires considerable development cost and technical know-how, and therefore they are used only in limited circumstances.

EXAMPLE: THE YEAR 2000

In 1970, a problem was posed: "What will the effect of different U.S. populations be on U.S. industries in the year 2000?" Given this rather nebulous topic, the decision was made to build a model of unit sales for 19 industries based on, among other things, population. A variety of approaches were considered and rejected:

1. Input-output analysis. (The researcher didn't know enough about it.)
2. Simultaneous equation regression models. (Insufficient time and budget.)
3. Index numbers. (Not enough experience with, too subjective.)

FIGURE 6–15
The Impact of Uncertain Predictors on Forecasting

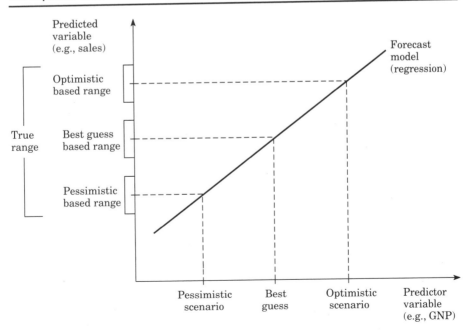

That left two good standbys: single-equation regression and polling of experts.

The major thrust was to use a single-equation model for each of the 19 industries. Also, 35 experts were asked to indicate what they thought would happen to sales in the 19 industries under different population assumptions (Howard and Lehmann, 1971). These judgments were used mainly to backstop the quantitative methods and helped eliminate unbelievable predictions. (Having believable predictions tends to increase the speed with which a consultant gets paid.)

Many potential regression models are available. There being no particular reason for choosing a particular one, a number were investigated (see Figure 6–16).

The results were then examined and the best model chosen. Almost without exception, the lagged models and first difference models produced "funny" results when extrapolated 30 years into the future based on the data used (1948–69 and 1959–69). In fact, the best results seemed to come from using the 1959–69 data on model 2:

$$\text{Sales} = B_0 + B_1(\text{POP}_t) + B_2\frac{\text{DI}_t}{\text{CPI}_t}$$

The resulting equations were then used for forecasting unit sales in the year 2000 under two population estimates and two disposable income estimates. The results clearly illustrate the frustration of forecasting 30 years into the future based on 11 years' worth of data. First, the supposedly low population estimate at the time was 266,281,000, a number that currently appears, if anything, high. Second, it is hard to believe that some of the projections will come true. The best example of this is automobiles, where the forecasts for the year 2000 based on the lower population and disposable income estimates were as follows:

	Unit Sales
Domestic	1.2 million
Imported	19 million

This result is hard to believe on two counts. First, it is difficult to project sales of 20 million cars in the year 2000 (at least cars as we know them today). Second, it seems unlikely that imported cars will be allowed (either by GM or other car manufacturers or the U.S. government) to so totally dominate the market. (It may be, however, that small cars will have such a dominant share.) This prediction is the result of the linear extrapolations of

FIGURE 6–16
Alternative Models of Sales as a Function of Population

1. $S_t = B_0 + B_1(POP_t)$

2. $S_t = B_0 + B_1(POP_t) + B_2\left(\dfrac{DI_t}{CPI_t}\right)$

3. $S_t = B_0 + B_1(POP_t) + B_2\left(\dfrac{DI_t}{CPI_t} \div POP_t\right)$

4. $S_t = B_0 + B_1(t) + B_2(POP_t) + B_3(DI_t/CPI_t)$

5. $S_t = B_0 + B_1(t) + B_2(POP_t) + B_3\left(\dfrac{DI_t}{CPI_t} \div POP_t\right)$

6. $S_t = B_0 + B_1(t) + B_2(POP_t)$

One-year lags

7. $S_t = B_0 + B_1(POP_{t-1})$

8. $S_t = B_0 + B_1(POP_{t-1}) + B_2(DI_{t-1}/CPI_{t-1})$

9. $S_t = B_0 + B_1(POP_{t-1}) + B_2\left(\dfrac{DI_t}{CPI_t} \div POP_{t-1}\right)$

10. $S_t = B_0 + B_1(t-1) + B_2(POP_{t-1}) + B_3(DI_{t-1}/CPI_{t-1})$

11. $S_t = B_0 + B_1(t-1) + B_2(POP_{t-1}) + B_3\left(\dfrac{DI_{t-1}}{CPI_{t-1}} \div POP_{t-1}\right)$

12. $S_t = B_0 + B_1(t-1) + B_2(POP_{t-1})$

Five-year lags

13. $S_t = B_0 + B_1(POP_{t-5})$

14. $S_t = B_0 + B_1(POP_{t-5}) + B_2(DI_{t-5}/CPI_{t-5})$

15. $S_t = B_0 + B_1(POP_{t-5}) + B_2\left(\dfrac{DI_{t-5}}{CPI_{t-5}} \div POP_{t-5}\right)$

16. $S_t = B_0 + B_1(t-5) + B_2(POP_{t-5}) + B_3(DI_{t-5}/CPI_{t-5})$

17. $S_t = B_0 + B_1(t-5) + B_2(POP_{t-5}) + B_3\left(\dfrac{DI_{t-5}}{CPI_{t-5}} \div POP_{t-5}\right)$

18. $S_t = B_0 + B_1(t-5) + B_2(POP_{t-5})$

First differences

19. $(S_t - S_{t-1}) = B_0 + B_1(POP_t - POP_{t-1})$

20. $(S_t - S_{t-1}) = B_0 + B_1(POP_t - POP_{t-1}) + B_2\left(\dfrac{DI_t}{CPI_t} - \dfrac{DI_{t-1}}{CPI_{t-1}}\right)$

21. $(S_t - S_{t-1}) = B_0 + B_1(POP_t - POP_{t-1}) + B_2\left(\dfrac{DI_t}{CPI_t} \div POP_t - \dfrac{DI_{t-1}}{CPI_{t-1}} \div POP_{t-1}\right)$

Logs*

22. $\log S_t = B_0 + B_1\log(POP_t) + B_2\log(DI_t/CPI_t)$

23. $\log S_t = B_0 + B_1\log(POP_t) + B_2\log\left(\dfrac{DI_t}{CPI_t} \div POP_t\right)$

Logs, one-year lags

24. $\log S_t = B_0 + B_1\log(POP_{t-1}) + B_2\log(DI_{t-1}/CPI_{t-1})$

25. $\log S_t = B_0 + B_1\log(POP_{t-1}) + B_2\log\left(\dfrac{DI_{t-1}}{CPI_{t-1}} \div POP_{t-1}\right)$

Logs, five-year lags

26. $\log S_t = B_0 + B_1\log(POP_{t-5}) + B_2\log(DI_{t-5}/CPI_{t-5})$

27. $\log S_t = B_0 + B_1\log\left(\dfrac{DI_{t-5}}{CPI_{t-5}} \div POP_{t-5}\right)$

S = Sales
POP = Population
DI = Disposable income
CPI = Total consumer price index
t = Time (year)
* This implies $S^t = B_0(POP_t)^{B_1}(DI_t/CPI_t)^{B_2}$

the past trend over a long period. While linear extrapolations work well in the short run, they tend to be off in the long run. The point, therefore, is that these estimates cannot be maintained with much certainty (Would you believe a confidence interval of zero to infinity?). That doesn't mean long-range forecasts aren't important; airports, utilities, and so forth, all need to plan many years into the future. It does mean that anyone doing long-range forecasting deserves credit for courage and some sympathy.

PRESENTATION OF FORECASTS

Forecasting Methods

The time horizon has a major effect on the appropriate forecasting method(s) to choose and the accuracy one can expect. Put bluntly, anything will do to predict next week (with exceptions—such as umbrellas), and nothing can predict 30 years ahead. The relation between the time horizon of the forecast and the method to be used can be summarized as follows:

Term of Forecast	"Best" Method
1. Short (less than 6 months)	Simple extrapolation
2. Medium (1–5 years)	Quantitative (regression)
3. Long (5–30 years)	Model building and mystic
4. Super long (30 years and up)	Flip a coin, no one knows

Expressed differently, it is difficult to say which techniques are good and which are bad because it often depends on the circumstances involved. Still, comparisons are useful, and the summary provided by Chambers, Mullick, and Smith (1974) is widely viewed as an excellent summary. A comparison of methods appears in Georgoff and Murdick (1986). Actual use of forecasting techniques varies by industry and user sophistication (Figure 6–17). Most forecasts are done by fairly simple methods with sales force composites, expert opinion, and naive extrapolation being the three most widely employed according to one survey (Dalrymple, 1987).

Using quantitative procedures may at times seem tedious. Still, quantitative methods are beneficial for several reasons including: (1) they simplify routine, repetitive situations, and (2) they force explicit statements of assumptions. When using quantitative procedures, it is best to use the following steps:

FIGURE 6–17
Forecasting Methods Usage

Method	Percent Using Regularly	Percent Using Occasionally
Qualitative		
Sales force	44.8%	17.2%
Executive opinion	37.3	22.4
Intentions	16.4	10.4
Industry survey	14.9	20.9
Quantitative		
Naive extrapolation	30.6	20.1
Moving average	20.9	10.4
Leading indicators	18.7	17.2
Regression	12.7	9.0
Econometric models	11.9	9.0
Exponential smoothing	11.2	11.9

Source: Douglas J. Dalrymple, "Sales Forecasting Practices: Results from a United States Survey." Reprinted with permission from the *International Journal of Forecasting* 3 (1987), p. 383.

1. *Graph the data if possible.* "A picture may be worth a thousand analyses." As an example of how important a picture can be, consider again the eight-year period example of Figure 6–10. Graphed, the data look like Figure 6–18. An interesting pattern thus emerges: two up periods, followed by a down period. While this pattern is only three cycles old, it suggests that a forecast in the 130 to 140 area for period 9 would be supportable. This pattern can be overlooked by simple number crunching.
2. *Do sensitivity analysis.* Only when a result seems to be stable over method and data points (e.g., drop one or two points and rerun the analysis), can the forecast be advanced with much conviction.
3. *Examine big "residuals."* By examining the characteristics of those periods (data points) when the forecast was bad, omitted variables can often be uncovered.
4. *Avoid silly precision.* This means rounding off the forecast and giving an honest plus or minus range. It also means recognizing that the use of a regression model and the 2 sigma (standard errors of estimate) rule gives a 95 percent confidence level only if (*a*) the model was correct, (*b*) the same model holds in the future, and (*c*) we know the values of the predictor variables with certainty. Since none of these is likely to be true (though when time is the predictor variable, *c* is true) it means the 2 sigma range underestimates uncertainty.

FIGURE 6–18
Plot of Sales Data Example

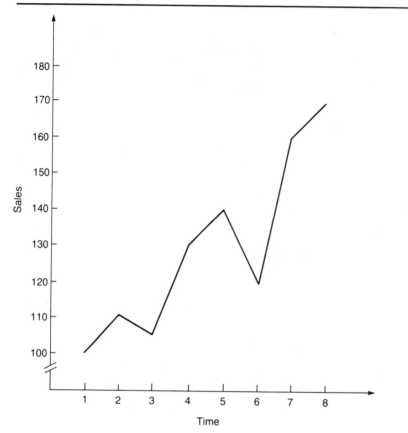

5. *Be tolerant of errors.* Expect the methods to improve one's odds of making a good forecast, not to guarantee them. Be suspicious of forecasts with very narrow ranges.
6. *Remember you will generally miss the turning points.* Quantitative (as well as qualitative) forecasting methods work well as long as the patterns that occurred in the past extend into the future. Whenever a major change occurs, however, most forecasts will be way off. Stated another way, most forecasting methods are generally useless for predicting major changes in the way the world operates (oil embargoes, changes in social values, and so on), and consequently the effects of these changes are not included in most forecasts.

Combining Forecasts

So far this chapter has described a number of forecasting methods and their strengths and weaknesses. In practice, when making an important forecast, it is both common and prudent to make several forecasts and then combine them. Put differently, the issue is not to decide which is the best forecast, but to create a forecast that combines the available forecasts. For example, in producing an industry forecast, one should generally do the following:

1. Plot the data and extrapolate. Normally, for mature industries a linear extrapolation will suffice (except for turning points, which it will miss), whereas for new industries a nonlinear procedure (such as the Bass model), which explicitly recognizes the eventual saturation level, is often useful.
2. Build a regression model that includes independent variables that are, as much as possible:
   • Good predictors.
   • Uncorrelated with each other.
   • Easy to forecast themselves.
      This model will generally include general economic variables (e.g., GNP, population) as well as industry variables (e.g., average price if it has been changing).
3. Collect forecasts available from others (e.g., security analysts).
4. Provide a subjective forecast based on consideration of likely future changes and their impact on sales.
5. Create a bottom-up forecast by summing up, for example, district managers' forecasts.

The results can then be summarized as in Figure 6–19. The range of these forecasts indicates the uncertainty faced. Moreover, deciding how to combine these forecasts forces one to make explicit assumptions.

A number of researchers have addressed the issue of the optimal way to combine forecasts (Gupta and Wilton, 1987, 1988). The best way is to weight forecasts based on their relative accuracy. Unless there is a great variation in accuracy, however, equal weighting works quite well.

Gaining Agreement

The previous sections have focused mainly on top-down forecasting, that is, a forecast made by a staff person. Bottom-up forecasts have various individuals (salespeople, division managers) make forecasts for their particular area and then aggregate these forecasts. Unfortunately, top-down and

FIGURE 6–19

Sample Format for Summarizing Forecasts

	Forecast		
Method	Pessimistic	Best Guess	Optimistic
1. Time series extrapolation	___	___	___
2. Regression model:			
Version A	___	___	___
Version B	___	___	___
3. Expert judgment:			
Expert A	___	___	___
Expert B	___	___	___
4. Own judgment	___	___	___
5. Bottom-up forecast	___	___	___

bottom-up forecasts rarely agree. The process of reaching agreement is both useful and frustrating.

In understanding bottom-up forecasts, it is useful to recognize that both personal incomes and budgets depend on the forecast. Personal incomes, especially of salespeople, are tied to quotas, which in turn are derived from forecasts. Therefore, a salesperson will tend to be conservative in his or her forecast to make the sales goal or quota easier to attain. By contrast, certain managers may overstate sales potential to gain a bigger budget. Thus, the bottom-up process, though based on the knowledge of those closest to the customer, may well produce a biased estimate. Therefore, total reliance on either bottom-up or top-down methods is generally a mistake.

Typically, then, forecasting may involve an iterative procedure where top-down and bottom-up forecasts are reconciled into a negotiated settlement.

Planning Assumptions

In constructing forecasts, a useful step is to formally state a number of "planning assumptions." These assumptions basically summarize key elements of the industry, competitors, and customer analysis, and include assumptions about:

1. Customers (identity, what they respond to).
2. Company (likely behavior in terms of, if relevant, pricing, advertising, new products, etc.).

3. Competitors (likely behavior including reactions to our behavior).
4. Industry (state of the economy, regulation, political climate, techno-logical changes).

These assumptions not only provide a useful summary of the earlier part of the plan, but also highlight what factors might explain deviations from forecasts and hence may be worth monitoring. While this step is required for regression model based forecasts, since the predictor variables must be identified and forecast, it is useful for organizing thinking for subjective forecasts as well.

SUMMARY

Since potential is a future-oriented concept, it is vital (but not always rec-ognized as such) to consider the impact of future changes in the market-place. These include all of the assumptions about the environment, including the economy, regulation, competitors, and so on. While many times such considerations may not materially affect the potential estimate or forecast, failure to consider them will almost ensure that some major turning points in a market will be missed. Since one of the major objectives of planning is to reduce surprises, at least a casual future scanning is strongly recommended.

In presenting forecasts, it is desirable to indicate the level of uncer-tainty involved. This requires recognition of uncertainty concerning market conditions (e.g., state of the economy) as well as uncertainty given a set of conditions. A simple form of such a presentation is shown in Figure 6–20.

One advantage of Figure 6–20 is that it highlights the key determi-nants of the forecast (often uncovered in a regression analysis) in the scen-arios in a nontechnical way. Also, by presenting both a best guess and low and high estimates (again, these can be based on a regression analysis by

FIGURE 6–20
A Format for Presenting Forecasts

Scenario	Low Estimate	Best Guess	High Estimate
Maximum potential (fast GNP growth, and so on)			
Best guess (moderate growth in GNP, and so on)			
Minimum potential (no growth in GNP, and so on)			

adding and subtracting standard errors from the best-guess prediction), the level of uncertainty is made clearer.

Finally, it is crucial to recognize that forecasting is a trying undertaking. Besides a sense of security and humor, the following are useful tools:

1. Understanding of:
   a. The problem.
   b. The situation.
2. Common sense.
3. Willingness to live with uncertainty. (False precision costs money since it doesn't encourage proper contingency planning.)
4. A number cruncher (the ability to use quantitative methods).
5. A coin. At some point in the forecasting process, a guess will need to be made. By using a coin, you can blame the result on someone or something else (e.g., a consultant, whom you can at least have the satisfaction of firing before your pink slip arrives).

APPENDIX 6A: TIME SERIES REGRESSION WITH SEASONAL FACTORS

Consider the following data on quarterly fuel oil shipments to the United Kingdom in 1964–66 (Figure 6A–1). In plotting this data, we see that there is, as expected, a very strong seasonal trend (Figure 6A–2). Ignoring the seasonal component would be a major error. (It would also produce significant autocorrelation.) Running four

FIGURE 6A–1
Fuel Oil Shipments to the United Kingdom

Quarter	Year	Sales
1	1964	210
2		120
3		140
4		260
1	1965	220
2		125
3		145
4		270
1	1966	225
2		128
3		149
4		275

FIGURE 6A–2

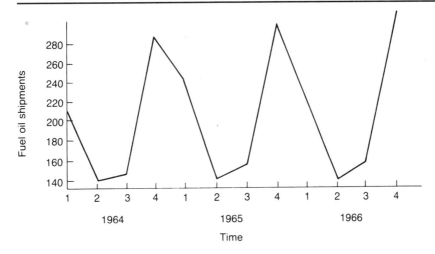

separate regressions is impractical because there would be only three observations per regression. It would be possible to deseasonalize the data before performing the regression, using an adjustment factor for each quarter such as

$$\frac{\text{Average sales for the particular quarter}}{\text{Average sales for all quarters}}$$

Possibly the most appealing approach, however, is to use dummy variables. This would consist of first creating ("dummying up") a variable for each of the four

FIGURE 6A–3

| Shipments | Time | Dummy Variables | | | |
		Winter	Spring	Summer	Fall
210	1	1	0	0	0
120	2	0	1	0	0
140	3	0	0	1	0
260	4	0	0	0	1
220	5	1	0	0	0
125	6	0	1	0	0
145	7	0	0	1	0
270	8	0	0	0	1
225	9	1	0	0	0
128	10	0	1	0	0
149	11	0	0	1	0
275	12	0	0	0	1

quarters (Figure 6A–3). The following equation would then be estimated by regression:

$$\text{Shipments} = B_0 + B_1 \text{ (Time)} + B_2 \text{ (Winter)} + B_3 \text{ (Spring)} + B_4 \text{ (Summer)}$$

Note that one of the possible dummy variables must be left out so the computer program will run. If all the independent variables are included, the independent variables are perfectly multicollinear. In this case, it is impossible to invert a key matrix, and the program will bomb. (Alternatively, we could drop the constant B_0 and retain all four dummy variables, if that were an option of the computer program being used.) In general, if a categorical variable has c categories, $c - 1$ dummy variables must be employed. Here, fall was excluded. This does not affect the final interpretation of the results, which are independent of the variable deleted. The results were:

$$B_0 = 256.5$$
$$B_1 = 1.468$$
$$B_2 = -45.6$$
$$B_3 = -141.1$$
$$B_4 = -122.2$$

Predictions for each of the quarters are thus:

Winter: Shipments $= B_0 + B_1 \text{ (Time)} + B_2(1) + B_3(0) + B_4(0)$
                    $= (B_0 + B_2) + B_1(\text{Time})$
                    $= 210 + 1.468 \text{ (Time)}$
Spring: Shipments $= (B_0 + B_3) + B_1 \text{ (Time)}$
                    $= 115.5 + 1.468 \text{ (Time)}$
Summer: Shipments $= (B_0 + B_4) + B_1 \text{ (Time)}$
                    $= 134.4 + 1.468 \text{ (Time)}$
Fall: Shipments $= B_0 + B_1 \text{ (Time)}$
                    $= 256.6 + 1.468 \text{ (Time)}$

The results are shown graphically as Figure 6A–4. The coefficients of the dummy variables are interpreted as the difference in the average value of the dependent variable between the category of the dummy variable and the category of the variable that has no dummy variable. Thus,

$$B_2 = \frac{210 + 220 + 225}{3} - \frac{260 + 270 + 275}{3} + 3(1.468)$$
$$= -50 + 3(1.468) = -45.6$$

Here the coefficients of the dummy variables indicate the difference in average sales between each quarter and the fall quarter. For example, average shipments in the spring are 45.6 less than shipments in the fall.

If this model were used to predict shipments in the second quarter of 1968, the best-guess prediction would then be

$$\text{Predicted shipments} = 115.5 + 1.468(18) = 142$$

FIGURE 6A–4

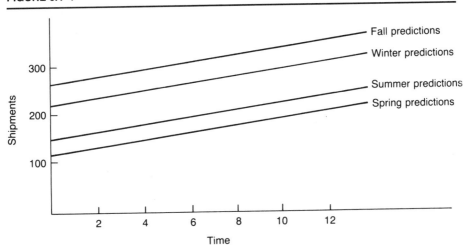

APPENDIX 6B: EPIDEMIC MODELS OF INITIAL SALES

A general form of the epidemic model is given by:

$$P(\text{Buy/Not previously bought}) + a + bF + c(1 - F) + dF(1 - F)$$

where F = Cumulative sales/Saturation level. Most popular diffusion models are a special case of this. For example, the Bass model assumes c and $d = 0$.
    The model used by Bass has the following form:

$$p(t) = p + \frac{q}{M}Y(t)$$

where

$p(t)$ = Probability of purchase given no previous purchase was made
$Y(t)$ = Total number who have tried
M = Total number of potential buyers (saturation level)
q = Parameter reflecting the rate of diffusion of the product
p = Initial probability of first-time purchase

Thus,

$$S(t) = [M - Y(t)]p(t)$$

$$= pM + [q - p]\,Y(t) - \frac{q}{M}[Y(t)]^2$$

The model can be estimated by running a regression of current versus past sales:

$$S(t) = c_0 + c_1 Y(t) + c_2 [Y(t)]^2$$

We can then solve for p, q, and M by letting $c_0 = pM$, $c_1 = [q - p]$, and $c_2 = -q/M$. As an example, we estimated the Bass model on annual workstation sales from 1984 to 1991. The resulting model was:

$$\text{Sales} = 13.67 + 0.90\ Y(t) - .00054\ [Y(t)]^2$$

Figure 6B–1 shows the forecast values, which are quite close to the actuals. The forecast for 1992 is

$$13.67 + 0.90(1008.72) - .00054(1008.72)^2 = 372.$$

The forecast of 372,000 units was essentially flat. (This ignores both the positive impact of lower prices and the negative impact of a depressed economy.) In terms of p, q, and M, by using the quadratic formula we get $M = 1,670,000$, $p = .0081$, and $q = .907$. This indicates a strong imitation effect (q is large), consistent with the generally higher imitation coefficients found for industrial goods.

The Bass model has fit past adoption patterns as well. For example, it correctly forecast a downturn in sales of color TVs in the late 1960s, something the "expert" forecasts at the major manufacturers failed to do because of their use of essentially linear extrapolation. Unfortunately, the model is sensitive to data points and therefore unreliable when only four or five data points (e.g., years of sales) are available. (Reasonable forecasts are obtainable when the results of past studies—essentially the average values of p and q—are combined with data-based estimates; Sultan, Farley, and Lehmann, 1990.) The simple models also ignore marketing variables. For example, the saturation level M probably depends on price, which often declines over time, and the purchase rate $p(t)$ depends on distribution, advertising, and so on. Also, estimating this model separately for major segments noticeably improves predictive power (Wind, Robertson, and Fraser, 1982). For a more complete treatment of this area, see Mahajan, Muller, and Bass (1990).

FIGURE 6B–1

Bass Model: Workstation Actual versus Predicted

Year	Workstation Sales (000s)	Y(t)	Predicted	Percent Error
1984	5	0	13.67	173%
1985	10	5	18.15	82%
1986	22	15	27.02	23%
1987	54.64	37	46.17	−16%
1988	104.71	91.64	91.44	−13%
1989	185.55	196.35	169.14	−9%
1990	255.00	381.90	277.57	9%
1991	371.82	636.90	365.56	−4%
1992		1,008.72	372	

While the Bass model of sales over time has some appealing behavioral justification, a variety of alternative models is available. These include:

1. *Exponential.* By assuming $S(t) = a + be^{-t}$, a curve projecting sales is derived.
2. *Weibull.* The Weibull distribution is widely used to predict product failure, and it is frequently used in marketing as an alternative to the Bass model. Usually, the Weibull and Bass models produce fairly similar results. The model is

$$S(e) = \frac{bt^{b-1}}{a} \exp \frac{(-t^b)}{a}$$

or

$$Y(t) = 1 - \exp \frac{(-t^b)}{a}$$

3. *Technological Substitution.* One interesting approach to projecting the impact of a new (and presumably better) technology is to examine the rate at which it replaces the old technology. The simplest of such models assume that eventually (at least for some segments) substitution will be complete. One model of the substitution process was developed by Fisher and Pry (1971) and discussed extensively by Cooper and Schendel (1976). The model is based on the assumption that the fraction (f) who will adopt the new technology is given by

$$\frac{df}{dt} = 2\alpha \frac{f}{(1 - f)}$$

This leads to

$$f = \tfrac{1}{2}[1 + tanh\ \alpha(t - t_0)]$$

The model has been shown to fit a number of situations, including open hearth versus Bessemer steel production, water- versus oil-based paints, and plastic versus metal in automobiles. Consequently, if one has a few years of data for a new product, one can separately forecast the fraction (f) who will use the new product and the size of the total market (new plus old), which may be essentially constant, and then estimate potential of the new product by multiplying f times total market. While this model obviously does not consider (a) changes in the marketing mixes of makers of the two product types, (b) increases in primary demand due to the properties of the new product, or (c) measurement issues such as appropriate units (e.g., pounds, dollars, number of applications), it still provides a useful benchmark for potential estimates. Fisher and Pry (1971) also observed the following:

- Sales of the old product may initially continue to expand and generally did.
- The time until the old product was replaced by the new as the sales leader was 5 to 14 years.

- The initial model of the new product was crude and expensive, which led to an underestimation of its potential.
- The new product "overpowers" the old market segment by segment rather than across the board.

REFERENCES

Armstrong, J. Scott; Roderick J. Brodie; and Shelby McIntyre. "Forecasting Methods for Marketing: Review of Empirical Research." *Singapore Marketing Review* 11 (1987), pp. 7–23.

Bass, Frank M. "A New Product Growth Model for Consumer Durables." *Management Science* 15 (January 1969), pp. 215–27.

Chambers, John C.; Satinder K. Mullick; and Donald D. Smith. "How to Choose the Right Forecasting Technique." *Harvard Business Review,* July–August 1971, pp. 45–74.

Bayus, Barry L., Saman Hong, and Russell P. Labe, Jr. "Developing and Using Forecasting Models of Consumer Durables: The Case of Color Television." *Journal of Product Innovation Management* 6, (1989), pp. 5–19.

Chambers, John C.; Satinder K. Mullick; and Donald D. Smith. *An Executive's Guide to Forecasting.* New York: John Wiley & Sons, 1974.

Cooper, Arnold C., and Dan Schendel. "Strategic Responses to Technological Threats." *Business Horizons,* February 1976, pp. 61–69.

Cox, William E., Jr., and George N. Havens. "Determination of Sales Potential's and Performance for an Industrial Goods Manufacturer." *Journal of Marketing Research* 14 (November 1977), pp. 574–78.

Cox, William E., Jr. *Industrial Marketing Research.* New York: Ronald Press, 1979.

Dalrymple, Douglas J. "Sales Forecasting Practices: Results from a United States Survey." *International Journal of Forecasting* 3, (1987), pp. 379–91.

Draper, N., and H. Smith. *Applied Regression Analysis.* New York: John Wiley & Sons, 1966.

Fisher, J. C., and R. H. Pry. "A Simple Substitution Model of Technological Threats." *Technological Forecasting and Social Change* 3 (1971), pp. 75–88.

Georgoff, David M., and Robert G. Murdick. "Manager's Guide to Forecasting." *Harvard Business Review,* January–February 1986, pp. 110–20.

Gupta, Sunil, and Peter C. Wilton. "Combination of Forecasts: An Extension." *Management Science* 33 (March 1987), pp. 356–72.

Gupta, Sunil, and Peter C. Wilton. "Combination of Economic Forecasts: An Odds–Matrix Approach." *Journal of Business and Economic Statistics* 8 (July 1988), pp. 373–79.

Howard, John A., and Donald R. Lehmann. "The Effect of Different Populations on Selected Industries in the Year 2000." Commission on Population Growth and the American Future, Research Reports, Vol. II, *Economic Aspects of Populations Change.* Ed. Elliot R. Morse and Ritchie H. Reed. Washington, D.C.: United States Commission on Population Growth and the American Future, 1971, pp. 145–58.

Hummel, Francis E. *Market and Sales Potentials.* New York: Ronald Press, 1961.

Lehmann, Donald R. *Market Research and Analysis.* Homewood, Ill.: Richard D. Irwin, 1989.

McLaughlin, Robert L. "The Breakthrough in Sales Forecasting." *Journal of Marketing* 27 (April 1963), pp. 46–54.

McLaughlin, Robert L., and J. J. Boyle. *Short–Term Forecasting.* Chicago: American Marketing Association, 1968.

Mahajan, Vijay, Eitan Muller, and Frank M. Bass. "New Product Diffusion Models in Marketing: A Review and Directions for Research," *Journal of Marketing* 54, (January 1990), pp. 1–26.

Pessemier, Edgar A. *Product Management.* New York: John Wiley & Sons, 1977.

Stern, Mark E. *Market Planning.* New York: McGraw-Hill, 1966.

Sultan, Fareena; John U. Farley; and Donald R. Lehmann. "A Meta-Analysis of Applications of Diffusion Models." *Journal of Marketing Research* 27 (1990), pp. 70–77.

Tull, Donald S., and Del I. Hawkins. *Marketing Research.* New York: Macmillan, 1976.

Urban, Glen L., and John R. Hauser. *Design and Marketing of New Products.* Englewood Cliffs, N.J.: Prentice Hall, 1980.

Wheelwright, Steven C., and Spyros Makridakis. *Forecasting Methods for Management.* New York: John Wiley & Sons, 1985.

Wildt, Albert R. "Estimating Models of Seasonal Market Response Using Dummy Variables." *Journal of Marketing Research* 14 (February 1977), pp. 34–41.

Wind, Yoram; Thomas S. Robertson; and Cynthia Fraser. "Industrial Product Diffusion by Market Segment." *Industrial Marketing Management* 11 (1982), pp. 1–8.

CHAPTER 7

ANALYSIS AND STRATEGY

OVERVIEW

Assuming one conscientiously completes the kinds of analysis discussed in the first six chapters, an obvious question is what next? Also assuming elegant analysis on its own is of limited pragmatic value, the obvious answer is to use it to select a reasonable set of objectives, strategies, and programs. Put simply, the purpose of the "homework" (analysis) is to do better on the "test" (strategy selection and implementation). By first thoroughly understanding the market—customers, competitors, industry environment, and future conditions—the product manager has the appropriate context within which objectives, strategies, and programs can be developed. In this chapter, we briefly discuss the selection of objectives, strategy, and programs (elements of the marketing mix). While we make some specific links between analysis and strategy, we assume readers will be able to see many of the connections on their own. For a much more complete treatment of marketing strategy, see Hulbert (1985).

ELEMENTS OF PRODUCT STRATEGY

A complete statement of a product strategy consists of seven parts:

1. Statement of the objective(s) the product should attain.
2. Selection of strategic alternative(s).
3. Selection of customer targets.
4. Choice of competitor targets.
5. Statement of the core strategy.
6. Description of the supporting marketing mix.
7. Description of the supporting functional programs.

The first two elements, the objectives and strategic alternatives, establish general direction. The next three elements, the selection of customer and competitor targets and a description of the core strategy, are the essence of the strategy. Taken together, they are often referred to as positioning, that is, how the product is to be differentiated from the competition in the minds of the target segments.

Finally, the supporting marketing mix and functional programs relate to the implementation of the strategy. These are vital elements of a strategy. Indeed, many managers (as well as coaches) believe it is at least as important to execute a strategy well as it is to select a good strategy. However, discussing developing marketing programs requires a major effort. Since this is not consistent with our objectives for this book (i.e., a short book focusing on the analyses needed to guide strategy and planning), we do not discuss marketing program options here.

A systematic approach to developing strategy helps to achieve the coordination and integration referred to earlier. There is a logical ordering to the aspects of the strategy; marketing mix decisions such as price and advertising logically occur *after* the basic strategy has been determined. For example, a strategy of a high-quality positioning to upscale customers such as that pursued by Ralph Lauren's Polo clothing line must be implemented by high price, exclusive distribution, and classy advertising to obtain consistency between the strategy and the implementation. Of course the process is to some extent circular, and occasionally an inspired program will influence the choice of objectives and strategy.

SETTING OBJECTIVES

A variety of objectives exist in an organization ranging from corporate to product to human resource objectives. We are concerned with the type that addresses the question, "Where do we want to go?" The answer to such a question differs depending on the level of the organization. At the corporate level, objectives related to return on investment, stock share price growth, and business mix as well as employee treatment (e.g., "a supportive work environment") are common. These, however, are not very useful for the marketing manager as they give little guidance for how to proceed at the product level.

Figure 7–1 represents how the different levels of objectives and strategies appear in an organization: a hierarchy of objectives. As can be seen, objectives at different levels of the organization must mesh to achieve the overall corporate objectives. The job of ensuring that individual product objectives "sum" to the organization objective usually falls to corporate

FIGURE 7-1
Hierarchy of Objectives

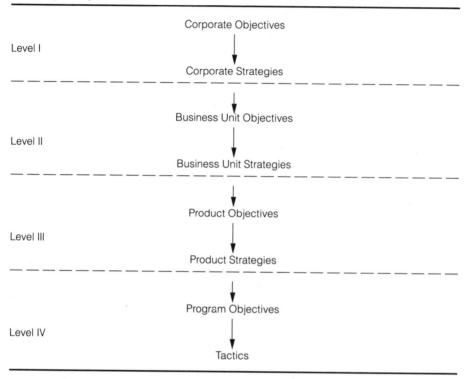

Level I	Corporate Objectives
	↓
	Corporate Strategies

Business Unit Objectives

Level II

Business Unit Strategies

Product Objectives

Level III

Product Strategies

Program Objectives

Level IV

Tactics

personnel who have the responsibility to negotiate both business unit and product objectives to achieve the overall objective.

In this book, we are primarily concerned with level III, the product objectives. The two areas in which specific product objectives are most commonly set are related to sales revenues or market share and profitability. This is an easy dichotomy to conceptualize because it is usually not possible to optimize both simultaneously. That is, the kinds of activities necessary to achieve an ambitious market share objective work against the satisfaction of an ambitious profit objective.

For example, to reach a market share objective, the usual short-term actions include reducing the price, increasing spending on advertising, expanding the sales force, and so forth. In other words, significant growth in share is, at the margin, achievable only by increasing expenditures or lowering profit margins per unit.

Of course many other types of objectives are also sometimes used (Figure 7–2). The basic dichotomy so far distinguishes between two types of *economic* objectives. While it can be argued that, in the long run, the only objective is cash flow (or stock price in the case of a publicly held corporation), other objectives are appropriate for the life of a typical marketing plan. For example, within the category of return-oriented economic objectives, cash-starved firms often try to maximize cash flow at the expense of profits (e.g., airlines in bankruptcy or highly leveraged LBOs) while other firms try to obtain "hard" currency (e.g., companies in inflation-prone or heavily controlled economies).

More importantly, a number of noneconomic (at least in the short run) objectives are also followed. It is difficult to find a large U.S. company in the early 1990s that has not made a major push for quality. Many firms have operationalized this direction in terms of customer satisfaction objectives (e.g., to increase satisfaction from 70 to 73 on a 100-point scale). Since satisfaction seems to directly affect future profits, of course, this ultimately leads to economic returns.

Similarly, many firms are concerned about a brand's reputation (image, equity) and have objectives to maintain or increase it. A brand is not only a collection of physical attributes and benefits but also a reservoir of value stemming from awareness, quality associations, brand personality, and

FIGURE 7–2
Possible Marketing Objectives

Economic (Firm Oriented)
  Volume oriented
    Sales
    Share
    Growth
  Return oriented
    Profit
    Cash flow
    "Hard" currency generation
    Return on assets, capital, etc.
Noneconomic (Outward Oriented)
  Customer oriented
    Quality/satisfaction
    Reputation/equity
  Behavior modification
    Shifting demand
    Acculturating/proselytizing
  Competitor punishment/signaling
    Decrease sales
    Decrease profits

loyalty. As such, it is an asset at least as important as the machinery to make the product or supply the service and the human resources associated with the product. However, while it is widely accepted that plant and equipment depreciate and need to be constantly maintained, brand value (perhaps because it is harder to measure) is often taken for granted. Tending and cultivating brand value should be a major focus of product management. Moreover, given day-to-day pressures, it should often be an explicit objective of the marketing program.

Less directly related to economic returns are objectives relating to shifting demand. While shifting demand to higher-margin products is obviously a means of increasing returns, shifting demand to more environmentally "friendly" products is less likely to produce economic returns (though it may help prevent regulation and so help maintain returns). Similarly, encouraging use of a particular product or lifestyle (e.g., acculturating/exposing the masses to art, promoting a religion or a way of life such as birth control) is a fairly common objective. In fact, this type of objective is often employed by not-for-profit or regulated organizations (e.g., transit authorities and utilities encouraging nonpeak usage, churches focusing on increasing members instead of revenues).

A final class of objectives has to do not with the firm's sales and returns but with those of its competitors. An objective of holding down competitors' results may be the direct consequence of a company-level enterprise competition. Alternatively it may be for the purpose of encouraging them to abandon the market (a common method for which is low pricing, sometimes referred to as predatory pricing). Finally, it may be to punish them for bad behavior and to signal them that they should cooperate (e.g., raise prices) in the future.

One can conceptualize the issue of selecting annual objectives as a mathematical programming problem. In such problems, there is some quantity to be optimized (maximized or minimized), subject to some constraints. Setting product objectives is analogous; the manager chooses which of share/sales or profits to maximize subject to some constraint of the other. Few senior managers would permit a growth objective without some consideration of its impact on the profits of the product. Likewise, profitability may be the main goal but subject to share maintenance or controlled decline (i.e., harvesting). The objective to be maximized might be called the *primary* objective, while the objectives acting as constraints could be termed *secondary* objectives.

There are several factors to consider when trying to assess which objective to pursue.

1. *The stage of the product life cycle (PLC).* Life cycle data come from the analysis of aggregate factors in the industry attractiveness analysis. Figure 7–3 shows how objectives might change over the life cycle. In the

FIGURE 7–3
Evolution of Objectives

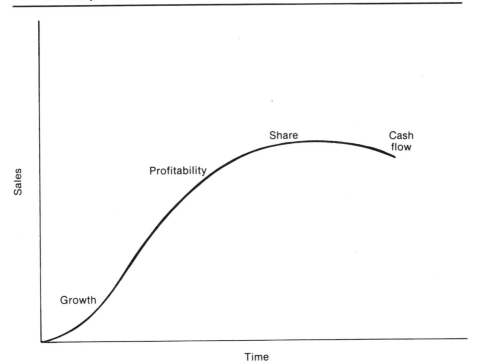

early stages of the PLC, the objective is generally to grow both in terms of sales and market share. The latter is particularly important as research evidence shows the long-run value of establishing an early position in a market (Urban, Carter, Gaskin, and Mucha, 1986). As the product moves toward maturity, more emphasis might be placed on profitability because high early expenses need to be recovered. In the maturity stage, competition among the remaining products is high; this competitive rivalry often stirs the combatants to market share wars (Coke versus Pepsi, McDonald's versus Burger King, for example). As the market declines, brands may be milked for profits or cash to put in more attractive products.

2. *The competition.* A competitor that is pursuing profits leaves an opening for more aggressive rivals. For example, the general malaise that hit the U.S. auto industry in the 1960s and early 1970s left significant openings for foreign competition. Companies that have been taken private through leveraged buyouts such as RJR/Nabisco often look to "fatten up" some businesses to sell them and raise cash to pay down debt. On the other hand, a well-heeled competitor striving to achieve market share gains may make it futile to strive for parity. IBM's thrust into the corporate segment of the PC market caused Apple to initially rethink its strategy both in terms of customer segments and product line rather than try to compete directly with IBM for share.

3. *Corporate decisions.* Often, the strategic business unit or division within which a product resides has a particular role for the product. For example, the well-known portfolio planning approach advocated by the Boston Consulting Group provides prescriptions for product objectives based on the growth rate of the market and the relative market share. Product managers may be told by a higher-level executive exactly what role the product will play in the portfolio. Thus, the selection of an objective may be outside the control of the product manager and may not always be that indicated by the situation analysis.

4. *Corporate or brand resources.* The amount of financial or other resources available may also restrict which objective can be selected. For example, the well-documented financial problems of Eastern Airlines made aggressive market share objectives impossible to finance. The problems also provided a convenient opportunity for other firms competing on the same routes, such as American and United, to improve their shares. The assessment of one's own resources is a vital component of the competitor analysis part of the situation analysis.

5. *Long-run objectives.* We discussed the conflict between market share and profitability in terms of the operating marketing plan, the focus of this book. However, often the long-run objective for a product, outside the scope of the annual plan, has significant impact on short-run objectives. For example, the aggressiveness of the Japanese and now the Koreans in pricing their products is often attributed to short-run market share objectives, which will ultimately produce longer-term profitability. For example, in automobiles and consumer electronics, Toyota and Sony are less aggressive in building share and more oriented toward profits than they were earlier.

Besides basing the selection of objectives on industry, customer, and competitive analysis, characteristics of good statements of objectives are:

1. They should be ambitious enough to be challenging subject to internal/external constraints. Objectives act as motivators. If regularly set too high, they are scorned by managers as being meaningless. If set too low, the organization does not achieve its potential. For example, Floating Point Systems, a manufacturer of scientific computers, consistently disappointed stock analysts with earnings that did not reach projections. As a result, the CEO set the objectives so low they could not be missed (*Business Week*, 1986). Clearly, such an objective-setting mechanism is inconsistent with what objectives are supposed to accomplish for an organization.

2. They should be attainable. While this may seem inconsistent with point 1, it really suggests good objectives involve a trade-off between hopes, high standards, and wishes as embodied in a fairly optimistic market potential estimate and the realities and likely results as assessed by a best-guess sales forecast.

3. They should have quantified standards of performance. In other words, every objective statement should include language such as "increase market share 2 share points."

4. They should have a time frame within which the objective should be achieved. Objectives are not open ended; for proper motivation and evaluation, a time frame must be set. For annual planning purposes, the planning period serves as an adequate time frame with perhaps quarterly checkpoints.

In sum, setting objectives involves choosing the appropriate objective, quantifying the objective with an amount, and setting a time frame for its achievement. It relies on the aspects of the situation analysis discussed in the previous sections of the book—the industry attractiveness analysis, the customer analysis, the competitor analysis, and the expected future conditions.

FUNCTIONS OF A STRATEGY

The primary purpose of a strategy is to provide a manager with the direction to follow in managing a business, and this book focuses on the product as the basic unit of analysis. This is consistent with a popular marketing organizational structure, the product management system, where each product manager's brand is treated as a separate business within the organization and the product manager is responsible for developing strategy.

For a strategy to prove workable, it must satisfy the following three requirements.

Help to Achieve Coordination

A workable strategy will help to *achieve coordination* between various functional areas of the organization. Different areas of the organization have different perspectives on how to make a product successful. The product manager would like to increase advertising spending. The sales manager would like more flexible pricing policies. Production personnel would like longer production runs and fewer products. Financial/accounting analysts require quantitative justification of all expenditures.

For a successful marketing effort, all functional areas must coordinate their activities. For example, suppose a computer manufacturer wishes to target a specific industry with unique product features. The image or "positioning" of the product is high quality and technological superiority. In such a case, the sales manager's flexible pricing orientation is inconsistent with the strategy. The production people may be upset with the segmentation approach because it means lower volume and more customization. The image-building activities of the advertising agency are difficult to evaluate in financial terms for the accounting personnel.

Clearly, a strategy that is not accepted, is poorly articulated, or is not well understood, cannot produce the necessary coordination. A strategy ensures that all members of the "team" are working together to achieve success for the product.

Define How to Allocate Resources

A strategy must *clearly define how resources are to be allocated.* At any level of the organization, resources are limited. Strategy is concerned with allocating the resources in a way that will achieve the goals set for the product. Often, some resource such as manufacturing or service capacity, sales force, time, money, and so forth will be more limited than others. In addition, these resources are often shared. For example, a single sales force often sells many different products. The lower the organizational level, the more resources are typically shared. Therefore, at the product level, it is essential the strategy provide clear guidance on allocation of resources across activities and other products.

Show How to Lead to a Superior Market Position

A strategy must *show how it can lead to a superior market position.* In Chapter 2, we showed how the definition of competitors is critical to market success. A good strategy takes cognizance of existing and potential competitors and their strengths/weaknesses (see Chapter 4). A marketing strategy is *competitively sensible* when it has the following qualities:

 a. It is something a competitor *cannot* do. This could be based on patent protection, extra capacity, or some other proprietary advantage.
 b. It is something a competitor *will choose not to do.* Often, smaller companies pursue small segments of the market in the hope that large companies will ignore them due to financial criteria. Federal Express overtook Emery in overnight delivery by buying its own planes, while Emery resisted such a move as it was focusing on

improving its return on employed capital at the time. Japanese car-makers had initial success by including options with the purchase price; American manufacturers refused to pursue that concept since they made high profit margins on the options.

c. It causes *a disadvantage for the competitor if it chooses to do it.* If brand A has lower costs of production than brand B, brand A has more pricing flexibility and brand B is at a disadvantage in a price war because its price floor is higher than A's.

d. It *causes us to gain if the competitor chooses to do it.* Campbell Soup ran a successful advertising campaign around the theme "Soup is good food." Such a theme is clearly generic and aimed at increasing soup consumption. Since Campbell has such a dominant position in the market, it benefits from such generic promotion. However, Heinz could not afford such a strategy as it would likely cause Campbell's sales to gain far more than Heinz.

In sum, a good marketing strategy eases the coordination between functional areas of the organization, helps allocate resources efficiently, and helps the product attain market leadership. A good strategy is also "competitive," that is, an action that provides advantage over the other organizations pursuing the same customers.

SELECTION OF STRATEGIC ALTERNATIVES

The choice of strategic alternatives logically follows the selection of a primary objective. This is really the first step in the development of the marketing strategy as it provides the broad guidelines for the ultimate strategy selected. The following paragraphs offer a way for the marketing manager to conceptualize strategic alternatives.

Figure 7–4 presents the economic objectives in a tree-like structure emanating from a box labeled "long-term profits." In other words, it is assumed that the long-run objective of any product is to maximize profits. However, given that assertion, we link the description of the alternatives to whether the primary annual planning objective is growth in sales/share or profitability. The options available to the marketing manager depend on the objective selected. If a manager chooses growth, the three main ways to achieve this growth are market penetration, market development strategies, and introduction of new products or extensions. Market penetration is oriented toward current or past customers; market development strategies are directed toward selling the current product to current noncustomers. The new product strategy may focus on either current customers or

FIGURE 7–4
Strategic Alternatives

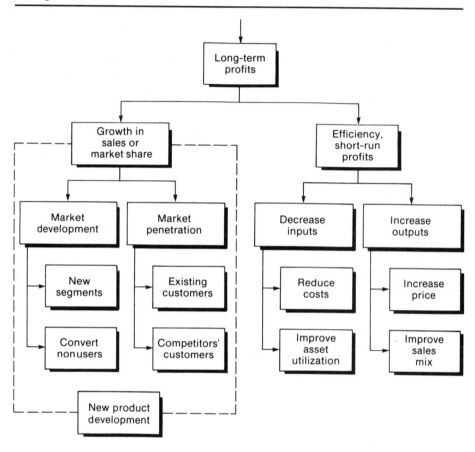

noncustomers and hence is related to but separate from the choice of target customers. If the profitability path is chosen, the primary focus is on either increasing outputs, that is, sales revenue from existing units sold, or decreasing inputs, that is, the factors of production. We discuss each of these in more detail below. Notice that choice of objectives may depend on time frame. A short time horizon and an ambitious sales goal push one toward market penetration strategies, since "loading" current customers with products can generally be done faster (e.g., through price promotions) than converting nonusers.

Increasing Sales/Market Share

Market Penetration Strategies

One way to increase market share or sales volume is by increasing the usage rate of existing customers. This could occur by getting them to use larger package sizes, consume more frequently, give us a larger share of their business, or a variety of other ways.

Many firms have successfully taken this tack. A classic example is Arm & Hammer baking soda, which has been marketed as useful in several ways, from freshening refrigerators and freezers to softening water and cleaning teeth. Banks try to get a larger share of a commercial customer's business by selling other services such as cash management. Coupons often try to induce customers to buy larger package sizes in the hope of increasing the consumption rate. In general, this is a good place to start because the customers being targeted are already familiar with the product and the company. In other words, marketing managers should always ask themselves: Is the actual consumption rate equal to the potential rate?

A second route to increasing sales or market share is to try to attract competitors' customers, that is, induce brand switching. This approach, while focusing on customers familiar with the product category, has several risks. First, the strategy can incur the wrath of a larger, more formidable competitor. Second, it may involve substantial use of sales promotion, which is costly. Third, a strategy to induce brand switching may call for comparative advertising, which is not only expensive but also risky in that, if poorly executed, it may call attention to the competitor's brand, particularly if the competitor is the market leader.

Market Development Strategies

These strategies are oriented toward noncustomers. One approach is to pursue nonusers in segments already being targeted. For example, if a word-processing system is being targeted to law firms, a development strategy would pursue those law firms that have not yet purchased a system. Essentially, this approach tries to tap remaining market potential from those segments identified as prime prospects.

A second approach is to enter new markets, that is, develop segments that have been previously ignored by the product category. A recent example of this strategy is from the antacid category where major manufacturers (e.g., Tums) have positioned their brands as not only a solution to stomach acid problems but also as a calcium additive for the diet. Thus, they are trying to draw in customers from a different benefit segment. Note that this also acts as a market penetration strategy because it may increase the consumption rate of those using the product already as an antacid.

Increasing Profitability

Increasing the Outputs

The easiest way to increase revenues from existing unit sales is to improve prices. This can be done in a variety of ways including increasing the list price, reducing discounts, reducing trade allowances, and so forth. One must be careful to do this, however, only within a range that the customer is price inelastic, or total revenues can fall.

The other way to increase revenues is to improve the sales mix. Often, the 80/20 rule of marketing holds with respect to a product line—20 percent of the products produce 80 percent of the sales volume or profits. In such an instance, it may make sense to reduce the product line to emphasize selling more of the profitable items. Alternatively, if we apply the rule to customers, we may want to deemphasize the unprofitable customers and concentrate our resources on those producing 80 percent of the profits.

Decreasing the Inputs

One way to decrease the inputs is through cost reduction. Obvious candidates for reduction are the fixed costs of marketing such as advertising, promotion, selling expenses, marketing research, and so forth. Unfortunately, reducing these may have adverse long-run effects. A possible danger in stressing variable cost reduction is that a reduction in the inputs can cause a commensurate reduction in the outputs if some of the variable cost reduction affects product quality.

A second way to decrease the inputs is to better use the assets at the disposal of the marketing manager. This might relate to keeping down the costs of inventories for a manufactured product and accounts receivable. Other related activities are running production equipment more efficiently and, at a more aggregate level, investing cash on hand in overnight interest-bearing securities.

Product managers choosing the profits branch of the tree must, of course, also choose customer targets. The probable approach for this objective would be to pursue current customers.

Summary

We have presented the broad strategic options available to a marketing manager in terms of strategic alternatives. A manager is not limited to either a "growth" or "profits" objective, and multiple objectives can be utilized simultaneously. For example, it is common to seek reductions in variable costs while pursuing market share gains. In addition, one may choose to both increase the consumption rate of current customers and introduce product line extensions.

The dilemma for the marketing manager is that several of the options may appear to be equally attractive. It is very difficult and expensive to successfully implement multiple strategic alternatives. The difficulty arises from the multiple positionings that may be required for the different alternatives. For example, to simultaneously obtain new customers and get current customers to buy more, different advertising campaigns may have to be run projecting different images. This can cause confusion among customers. Expenses increase because multiple strategies inhibit the ability to get economies of scale from advertising copy, increase the use of more expensive (in aggregate) spot TV versus national, and so forth. Thus, there is pressure on the marketing manager to select a subset of the options available and concentrate resources on them.

The choice of which options to pursue is aided by the situation analysis. Three key criteria for evaluating strategic alternative options are:

1. Size/growth of the segment. An important part of the customer analysis section of the situation analysis described in Chapter 5 focuses on exactly this—which customer groups are growing and how fast?

2. Opportunities for obtaining competitive advantage. In the competitor analysis, we assess competitor marketing strategies indicating which market segments they are pursuing and their claimed competitive advantages, the resources they can put into the market, and their likely future marketing strategies.

3. Resources available to penetrate the segment. This is covered in the self-analysis part of the assessment of competition.

CHOICE OF CUSTOMER TARGETS

As mentioned above, positioning entails a specific statement of how the product is different from the competition in the minds of a specific set of customers. Therefore, positioning encompasses: (1) customer targets, (2) competitor targets, and (3) some product feature(s) by which the differentiation will occur.

The choice of which customer group(s) to target follows immediately from the specification of the strategic alternatives. If the profit route is taken, then the customer targets are those of the current strategy, for example, women over the age of 35, or law firms. The task is similar for any of the growth alternatives. For the penetration–own customers and development–nonusers strategies, the customers or noncustomers of the current strategy would again be selected. For the penetration–competitor's customers strategy, the specific descriptors of those customers would be used. Finally, for the development–new segments strategy, the descriptors from the new segments chosen would be specified.

CHOICE OF COMPETITOR TARGETS

Even if the competition is not explicitly mentioned in any of the product's communication programs, it is still important to consider which competitors are the primary targets of the strategy. For a penetration strategy (stealing competitors' customers), this should be a straightforward result of the strategy, as the decision to pursue that strategic alternative should be made in conjunction with the analysis of which competitor's customers are the most easily pried away. However, all the strategic alternatives at least implicitly involve competition through the necessity of positioning the product *against* major competitors.

Positioning involves some prioritization of the competitors, both direct and indirect (see Chapter 2). Again, the chief source of information about this choice is the situation analysis where the strengths and weaknesses of the competition have been detailed. Additional insight can be gained from literature on marketing "warfare" (see, for example, Ries and Trout, 1986). Market leaders often take defensive steps and therefore focus on the strong second competitor and perhaps the third one. The followers in the market take different competitor stances depending on their market share relative to the leader. A strong second might focus on offensive warfare and target the leader. Weak followers often try to avoid the major competitors and seek market niches that have either few or weak rivals. For example, a recent trend in banking is to be a banking "boutique" offering customized services to individuals with a high net worth, thus avoiding competing with the large, full-service banks.

THE CORE STRATEGY

The core strategy defines the differential advantage that is to be communicated to the target customers. One categorization is basically economic and divides advantages into two basic categories (Porter, 1986):

1. Cost/price differential advantage.
2. Differentiation on product offering/service features.

In other words, you either have to have a lower price that can only be supported in the long run with lower costs or you have to be better on some element of the product offering. While evidence suggests these are not mutually exclusive alternatives (Hill, 1988; Phillips, Chang, and Buzzell, 1983), this dichotomy provides a useful framework for discussion.

As several examples will show, being stuck in the middle can be disastrous. Sears has been trying for years to upgrade its clothing department to a fashion image, which is very difficult when one can purchase power tools in the same store. Its decision to have "every day low prices" was a clear move toward one end of the positioning continuum. People's Express was a very successful, low-cost/price airline whose image was no-frills. It failed when it tried to expand its routes and service and began competing with United, American, and so forth, which had better, well-established reputations.

Cost/Price Strategy

A low-price differentiation strategy can be very successful. Wal-Mart made Sam Walton the richest man in the United States. Iowa Beef is a very successful meat packer that pays significant attention to cost cutting. Japanese firms have been successful through attention to low-cost production in the semiconductor industry; now they are being overtaken by firms in Taiwan, Singapore, and so on.

However, few firms have the size, capital, or other resources to be the low-cost manufacturer or service provider. As a result, marketing managers must constantly seek a point of difference that will induce customers to purchase when comparing their product to the competitor's.

To successfully implement the low-cost/price strategy, several activities must be pursued that are consistent with the experience curve phenomenon. First, a high volume of a single product or family of products should be produced. This focused production hastens the descent along the cost-reduction curve. These cost reductions must also be continuously pursued. Second, investment is focused on efficient facilities and market share. Finally, control focuses on cost; this applies to manufacturing products, delivering services, or implementing activities such as advertising or promotion.

Certain risks are associated with this strategy, however. One is that customer tastes shift so the product being produced in high quantity is not desired any more (e.g., Atari and videogames before the Nintendo era). A second is that technological shifts either make it easier for competitors to have the same costs or make the product obsolete. Competitors could also leapfrog in cost cutting, which eliminates this differential advantage.

Nonprice Strategy

The nonprice differential advantage is the product characteristic that allows the manager to obtain a price higher than the price that would be obtained under perfect competition. As students of microeconomics know, with many suppliers of undifferentiated commodities, the market price is marginal cost. Therefore, the differential advantage is intended to create added value in the minds of the customers that enables the producer to obtain a higher price than the pure competition case; that is, a significant differential advantage means customers focus on product benefits rather than price.

How can a differential advantage be obtained? Levitt (1986) attempts to structure thinking about the problem using the concept of the "total" product as in Figure 7–5. His point is that the product is much broader than most marketing managers realize and the way to differentiate is to consider those "other" aspects of the product beyond the actual product or service itself.

For example, consider an automobile dealership. With respect to Figure 7–5, the generic product is the car. This can usually be purchased at several local dealers, so some differentiation is necessary. However, customers don't just buy a car from a dealer; they also have certain expectations about other services that normally come with the purchase. Customers expect financing capabilities, a service department, and so forth. Again, some differentiation is still necessary because most dealers supply the "expected" product. Real differential advantages can exist, however, if the dealer considers offering services *beyond* what is expected (i.e., the "augmented" product). For example, successful dealers train their salespeople to send birthday cards to buyers, remember their first names when the car is being serviced, and so forth. In the service area, some wash cars, keep appointments, provide loaner cars, and so on.

FIGURE 7–5
Total Product Concept

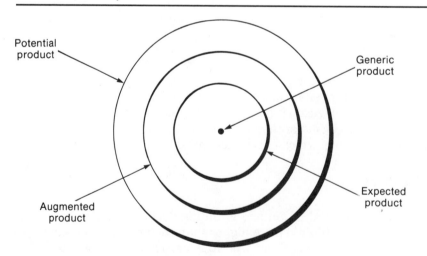

Levitt's point is that differential advantages are obtained by going beyond what customers expect into the realm of unanticipated product benefits. While it may take some creative thinking, one should move away from asking, "How can I make this product different?" to thinking "What am I selling?" By focusing on what customers are buying, that is, benefits, marketers can better determine how to make their product or service different from the competition.

Porter (1986) discusses four major areas where organizations can obtain differential advantage. These are just as applicable at the specific product or service level:

1. *Inbound logistics.* This translates into buying the highest-quality materials for a manufactured good or hiring the best people for a service. Steinway is well known for buying only the most expensive materials for its pianos; Singapore Airlines is the most selective in the airline business for its flight attendants and has a strong reputation for in-flight service.

2. *Operations.* In this case, the manufacturing process or service operation is where differentiation occurs. Perdue has the most efficient and technologically advanced process for growing chickens, for example. Delta has established a sound reputation for luggage handling, ticketing, and so forth.

3. *Outbound logistics.* In this case, the delivery system is the key. Federal Express is a prime example (it also fits in the operations category). Premier Industrial Corporation sells mundane items like nuts and bolts. However, this firm makes more money than competitors partly because it is willing to ship order sizes as small as one screw (at a higher price, of course), while competitors have minimum order sizes.

4. *Marketing/sales.* One type of differential advantage in this category is after-sales service. Timken (bearings), Caterpillar (farm equipment), and other firms differentiate their products by having better service and technical advice than competitors. A second type of marketing advantage recognizes that product differences are not the only way to gain advantage. Perceptual differences often are just as important. Thus, Miller in its "Miller Time" ad, Marlboro cigarettes, and many other consumer products focus largely on obtaining a perceived product difference based on image. Attempts to differentiate perceptually usually are successful in product categories where the products are very similar or where the quality of the product is hard to assess (e.g., life insurance policies).

Perceptual mapping, the research technique briefly described in Chapter 2 in a competitor definition context, has been extensively used by marketing managers to assess the current position of brands relative to customer and competitor targets and to help determine if repositioning can help. Figure 7–6 shows what is called a *joint space* because it not only indicates brand locations versus competition, but it also displays what are called *ideal points,* which are clusters of households based on their estimated preferred bundle of the attributes represented by the two axes. Note that the map incorporates all three aspects of positioning. Customers are represented by the ideal points (the segments are numbered according to size), competitors are also located on the map, and the differential advantage can be assessed using the brand attributes represented by the axes.

FIGURE 7–6
Joint Space for Colas

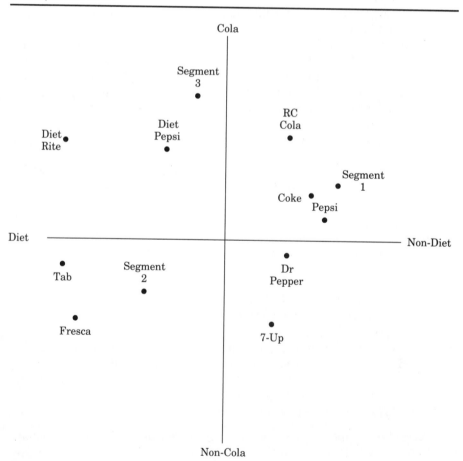

Consider the perspective of RC Cola. It is perceived as a nondiet cola, but is equidistant from segment 1, which is close to Coke and Pepsi, and segment 3, which seems to want a cola but a more diet variety. RC can position itself more to the mainstream but encounter heavy competition from Coke and Pepsi or it can go to segment 3 with a "lighter" image where it has fewer competitors. However, this latter group is also the smallest. Thus, the method helps to make the assessment of a differential advantage, particularly one that focuses on perceptions, simpler to marketing managers.

The requirements for a nonprice-differential-advantage core strategy are naturally quite different from those for a cost/price strategy. First, the strategy implies searching for continuous product improvements to maintain the differential advantage. For example, mail-order personal computer manufacturers first differentiated themselves solely on price, then third-party service contracts, and now 24-hour hot lines for service or other questions. The need for continuous product improvements implies a commitment to expenditures on marketing research and on R&D. Flexibility is also needed both in production and management to keep up with changes in customer tastes and competition. Finally, it is becoming common for customers of high-quality products and services to demand increased levels of personal services. For example, some hospitals offer accommodations for relatives of patients.

There are also risks in the differential advantage strategy. First, the cost/price differential may become so great that customers are willing to pay less to get less. Perhaps the biggest problem is that the differential disappears by imitation. Witness the quick adoption of frequent flier programs by almost all the major international airlines. Who remembers or cares that American was the first with such a program?

EXAMPLE

Consider Hewlett-Packard's 80386-chip personal computer as of late 1989. A possible strategy might look like the following. Underlying these statements are detailed analyses of the industry, competition, company, customers, and expected future conditions.

Objective: The objective for 1990 is to increase HP's share of the 80386-based PC market from 2 percent to 4 percent. Consistent with the customer's shifts to distributed computing, the corporate priority is shifting from mini- to microcomputers. Further, HP's engineering skills and financial strength are well suited to the market. Unlike the 808X and 80286 markets, the 80386 market still appears to reward technical excellence, is expected to grow strongly, and has room for another major player.

Strategy: Since market share is the objective, either market penetration or development are the two main alternatives. One approach is to focus on market penetration (i.e., current and competitor customers). The former consists largely of the scientific segment (i.e., universities, R&D applications, etc.). The scientific segment is expected to grow 26 percent in 1990 and already has high regard for HP's name and products. In addition, HP already has good relationships with the segment's large buyers. The competitor customers consist largely of business customers. This segment is attractive since (1) it will provide HP with credibility as a major PC manufacturer, (2) it will help create leverage with major PC retailers for obtaining shelf space, and (3) relationships with such customers can be long-lasting and lucrative.

Customer targets:

Scientific users (current customers): Engineers, scientists, manufacturing personnel.

Business users (competitor customers): Fortune 1,000 firms.

Competitor targets: For both segments, the major competitors are IBM and Compaq.

Core strategy: The core strategy will emphasize product quality over price. The two major platforms of this strategy are performance and safety. The performance aspect will be reinforced not only by CPU speed and other physical attributes but also by relying on HP's long-standing reputation for engineering excellence such as has been manifested by their calculators and Laserjet printers. Thus, HP's PCs can effectively and believably be positioned as higher performance than IBM and of at least equal performance to Compaq. Safety has two dimensions. First, IBM's introduction of the Microchannel system architecture in turn raised some doubt about its commitment to compatibility, which has somewhat decreased IBM's reputation as the safest computer to purchase. Second, relative to Compaq, which is small in comparison, HP is perceived as being much more likely to succeed in the long term. Positioning to the scientific community will stress performance primarily and safety as a secondary attribute; positioning to the Fortune 1,000 will stress safety first and performance second.

SUMMARY

In this chapter, we discussed development of the marketing strategy. The complete marketing strategy includes objectives, broad guidelines for the strategy, product positioning, and integration of both marketing mix elements and other functional areas such as finance and operations. As was noted repeatedly, the strategy follows directly from the plan's situation analysis section. Once the "homework" has been done, the elements of the strategy become much clearer than if one had just started with the problem of developing a strategy in the absence of market information.

As noted earlier, one benefit of the process advocated here is that it facilitates coordination between the various marketing mix elements and other functional areas such as finance and operations. An illustration shows how failure to integrate the mix can lead to sales problems.

LaCoste is known for its line of sports shirts featuring its signature alligator (actually, a crocodile, as it is named for Henri Lacoste, the French tennis player of the 1920s known as "Le Croc"). These shirts were an enormous financial success for the parent company, General Mills, in the 1970s and were obviously positioned as fashion items. The marketing mix was well integrated: the distribution channels were only upscale department stores such as Macy's, the shirts came in many attractive colors, and they were priced high. However, the firm subsequently made a critical error: it expanded the distribution channels to include discount stores, and the shirts began showing up in off-price retailers such as Marshall's. Clearly, this was an inconsistency in the minds of customers as "anyone" could now own a LaCoste shirt as opposed to its prior more exclusive image. Other shirts such as Polo by Ralph Lauren became the prestige shirt to own. Sales suffered and LaCoste was sold by General Mills in 1986.

As shown in Figure 7–1, the advocated approach is "top down" in that the product objectives imply a strategy that further implies tactics. The figure also gives some guidance on how to approach repairing a strategy if objectives are apparently not met. For example, it is possible that after six months, the market share goal set for the annual plan can appear to be unrealistic. In such a situation, where should the manager start, "bottom up" (i.e., with the tactics) or "top down," with the strategy?

The answer to this question is clear. Since the marketing mix or tactics implement the strategy, the first question to answer, in Peter Drucker's terms, should be, Am I doing things right? Is the advertising targeted to the right audience? Am I spending enough on promotion? Is the price right? In other words, while the strategy is determined "top down," attempts to fix a strategy should be made "bottom up," that is, the execution should be examined before the strategy. If the strategy is changed, all else below it in the hierarchy could be changed as well since the marketing mix is dependent on the strategy.

A FINAL NOTE

As is often stated (e.g., Lehmann, 1989, chap. 2), unless the odds of making a good decision change as the result of information being collected, then the information has no value. The basic premise of this book is that information about the business environment *has* value to marketing managers in competitive markets. We have attempted to be explicit about the information and analyses necessary to create value out of the marketing planning activity.

The major analyses we advocate are:

1. *Sales analysis*—a detailed look at the product's own sales record to analyze sales and market share differences between geographic regions, product sizes, and so on.
2. *Industry analysis*—an assessment of basic industry and environmental factors affecting the product.
3. *Customer analysis*—an examination of the basic aspects of customer behavior in terms of who they are and why and how they buy.
4. *Competitor analysis*—information collected to keep abreast of competitor activities and to enable the manager to predict future competitor product strategies.
5. *Market potential and forecasting*—essential, forward-looking activities that help the manager determine appropriate strategic objectives for the product.

Whether better decisions are made as a result of the procedures recommended in this book is difficult to measure since we do not know what would have happened otherwise. However, the mere exercise of collecting and analyzing the data is worthwhile for keeping in touch with rapidly changing markets even if better decisions do not immediately result. Put differently, homework does not always help, but even intellectually gifted students or executives are, in general, better off when they do it.

REFERENCES

"Floating Point Adjusts Its Sights—Downward." *Business Week,* September 8, 1986.

Hill, C. W. L. "Differentiation vs. Low Cost of Differentiation and Low Cost: A Contingency Framework." *Academy of Management Review* 13, no. 3 (1988), pp. 401–12.

Hulbert, James M. *Marketing: A Strategic Perspective.* Katonah, N.Y.: Impact Planning Group, 1985.

Lehmann, Donald R. *Market Research and Analysis,* 3rd ed. Homewood, Ill.: Richard D. Irwin, 1989.

Levitt, Theodore. *The Marketing Imagination.* New York: Free Press, 1986.

Phillips, L. W.; D. R. Chang; and R. D. Buzzell. "Product Quality, Cost Position, and Business Performance: A Test of Some Key Hypotheses." *Journal of Marketing* 47, (January 1983), pp. 26–43.

Porter, Michael E. *Competitive Advantage.* New York: Free Press, 1986.

Ries, Al, and Jack Trout. *Marketing Warfare.* New York: McGraw-Hill, 1986.

Urban, Glen L.; Theresa Carter; Steven Gaskin; and Zofia Mucha. "Market Share Rewards to Pioneering Brands: An Empirical Analysis and Strategic Implications." *Management Science* 32 (Winter 1986), pp. 645–59.

INDEX